'Since 9/11 acts of hate directed at Muslim communities have become one of contemporary society's most significant social issues. Drawing upon their own ground-breaking research, renowned experts Zempi and Chakraborti have produced a superb work that details the harms caused by Islamophobic faith hate targeted against veiled women. Their findings, brilliantly outlined here, offer new and important insights into the nature and impact of gendered aspects of Islamophobia and exemplify why *Islamophobia, Victimisation and the Veil* will become *the* key text for scholars and practitioners working in this area.' – Jon Garland, University of Surrey, UK

'Zempi and Chakraborti have produced a timely, insightful and authoritative analysis of the nexus between Islamophobia, visibility, victimisation and discourses of the veil. By interrogating the veil as a marker of Muslim 'otherness' they expose how popular stereotypes contribute to intolerance towards veiled Muslim women but also to global relations between Islam and the West. They skilfully blend cutting-edge empirical research with larger critiques of vulnerability and identity to offer a much-needed, accessible and unique analysis of the gendered dimension of Islamophobic victimisation.' – Gail Mason, University of Sydney, Australia

'As contemporary hate crime scholarship continues to flourish in Britain, with this book Zempi and Chakraborti have made a significant contribution to our knowledge and understanding of an issue hitherto largely underexplored by the existing literature. There is a wealth of knowledge contained within this accessible volume, and given current political and social discourses, should be read by academics, policymakers, and practitioners alike.' – Nathan Hall, University of Portsmouth, UK

DOI: 10.1057/9781137356154.0001

Other Palgrave Pivot titles

Marian Duggan and Vicky Heap: **Administrating Victimization: The Politics of Anti-Social Behaviour and Hate Crime Policy**

Pamela J. Stewart and Andrew J. Strathern: **Working in the Field: Anthropological Experiences across the World**

Audrey Foster Gwendolyn: **Hoarders, Doomsday Preppers, and the Culture of Apocalypse**

Sue Ellen Henry: **Children's Bodies in Schools: Corporeal Performances of Social Class**

Max J. Skidmore: **Maligned Presidents: The Late 19th Century**

Lynée Lewis Gaillet and Letizia Guglielmo: **Scholarly Publication in a Changing Academic Landscape**

Owen Anderson: **Reason and Faith in Early Princeton: Piety and the Knowledge of God**

Mark L. Robinson: **Marketing Big Oil: Brand Lessons from the World's Largest Companies**

Nicholas Robinette: **Realism, Form and the Postcolonial Novel**

Andreosso-O'Callaghan, Bernadette, Jacques Jaussaud, and Maria Bruna Zolin (editors): **Economic Integration in Asia: Towards the Delineation of a Sustainable Path**

Umut Özkırımlı: **The Making of a Protest Movement in Turkey: #occupygezi**

Ilan Bijaoui: **The Economic Reconciliation Process: Middle Eastern Populations in Conflict**

Leandro Rodriguez Medina: **The Circulation of European Knowledge: Niklas Luhmann in the Hispanic Americas**

Terje Rasmussen: **Personal Media and Everyday Life: A Networked Lifeworld**

Nikolay Anguelov: **Policy and Political Theory in Trade Practices: Multinational Corporations and Global Governments**

Sirpa Salenius: **Rose Elizabeth Cleveland: First Lady and Literary Scholar**

Sten Vikner and Eva Engels: **Scandinavian Object Shift and Optimality Theory**

Chris Rumford: **Cosmopolitan Borders**

Majid Yar: **The Cultural Imaginary of the Internet: Virtual Utopias and Dystopias**

Vanita Sundaram: **Preventing Youth Violence: Rethinking the Role of Gender and Schools**

Giampaolo Viglia: **Pricing, Online Marketing Behavior, and Analytics**

Nicos Christodoulakis: **Germany's War Debt to Greece: A Burden Unsettled**

Volker H. Schmidt: **Global Modernity. A Conceptual Sketch**

Mayesha Alam: **Women and Transitional Justice: Progress and Persistent Challenges in Retributive and Restorative Processes**

Rosemary Gaby: **Open-Air Shakespeare: Under Australian Skies**

DOI: 10.1057/9781137356154.0001

palgrave▸pivot

Islamophobia, Victimisation and the Veil

▶

Irene Zempi
University Tutor, University of Leicester, UK

and

Neil Chakraborti
Reader in Criminology, University of Leicester, UK

DOI: 10.1057/9781137356154.0001

First published 2014 by
PALGRAVE MACMILLAN

Palgrave Macmillan in the UK is an imprint of Macmillan Publishers Limited, registered in England, company number 785998, of Houndmills, Basingstoke, Hampshire RG21 6XS.

Palgrave Macmillan in the US is a division of St Martin's Press LLC, 175 Fifth Avenue, New York, NY 10010.

Palgrave Macmillan is the global academic imprint of the above companies and has companies and representatives throughout the world.

Palgrave® and Macmillan® are registered trademarks in the United States, the United Kingdom, Europe and other countries

ISBN: 978–1–137–35616–1 EPUB
ISBN: 978–1–137–35615–4 PDF
ISBN: 978–1–137–35614–7 Hardback

This book is printed on paper suitable for recycling and made from fully managed and sustained forest sources. Logging, pulping and manufacturing processes are expected to conform to the environmental regulations of the country of origin.

A catalogue record for this book is available from the British Library.

A catalog record for this book is available from the Library of Congress.

www.palgrave.com/pivot

DOI: 10.1057/9781137356154

▶ *This is dedicated to the women who took part in this research and who were brave enough to share their experiences of Islamophobic victimisation.*

DOI: 10.1057/9781137356154.0001

Contents

DOI: 10.1057/9781137356154.0001

About the Authors

Irene Zempi is University Tutor at the Department of Criminology, University of Leicester, UK. She is also a member of the Advisory Committee for the Measuring Anti-Muslim Attacks Project organised by Faith Matters, a non-profit organisation which hopes to show the scale of the problem of Islamophobia and provide support for victims.

Neil Chakraborti is Reader in Criminology at the University of Leicester, UK and Adjunct Professor at the University of Ontario, Canada. He has researched and published widely within the fields of hate crime, victimisation and policing diversity. He is part of the editorial board of the *British Journal of Criminology*, is Chair of Research at the Board of Trustees for the Howard League for Penal Reform, and is Director of the Leicester Centre for Hate Studies.

palgrave▶pivot

www.palgrave.com/pivot

Introduction

Zempi, Irene and Neil Chakraborti. *Islamophobia, Victimisation and the Veil.* Basingstoke: Palgrave Macmillan, 2014. DOI: 10.1057/978113735614.0003.

▶

'I'm walking down the road and people look at me like they've seen an alien'.

Alima, 20 years old

'People avoid us because if they are near us they might be contaminated. This is making us feel as if we are dirty'.

Focus group participant

'Ripping my veil off was a very personal attack. It felt like a sexual attack'.

Haleemah, 32 years old

'Everything is a prison now. That's what it is, my life has become like a prison; everywhere is a prison. I'm forced to stay in my home so they have made me a prisoner. They are oppressing me'.

Maha, 40 years old

These comments exemplify the vulnerability of Muslim women who wear the niqab (face covering) as actual and potential victims of Islamophobia and highlight the cumulative impact of this type of victimisation upon them. As we shall see, the visibility of the niqab (hereafter 'the veil') marks Muslim women as particularly vulnerable to anti-Muslim attacks in the public sphere. Indeed, the wearing of the veil has come under much media, political and public scrutiny in the UK and elsewhere in the West in a post-9/11 climate. Within this framework, the veil is seen as a marker of gender inequality. As such, veiled Muslim women are routinely perceived as oppressed and subjugated, whilst Islam is understood as a misogynist and patriarchal religion. The wearing of the veil is not only synonymous with gender oppression but also with Islamist terrorism and a lack of integration. In this regard, it is perceived as a danger to public safety on the basis that the covering of the face hinders identification. The wearing of the veil is also understood as a marker of segregation on the basis that veiled Muslim women refuse to integrate into Western society. Taken together, these stereotypes provide the justification for Islamophobic attacks against veiled Muslim women as a means of responding to the multiple 'threats' of the veil as a symbol of gender inequality, religious fundamentalism and self-segregation.

There is a growing body of literature which suggests that veiled Muslim women are 'ideal' targets for those seeking to attack a symbol of Islam (see, for example, Allen, Isakjee and Young, 2013; Githens-Mazer and Lambert, 2010). However, despite the vulnerability of veiled Muslim

DOI: 10.1057/9781137356154.0003

women as actual and potential victims of Islamophobia, the nature and wider harms associated with this victimisation remain 'invisible'. As with other forms of hate crime, victims of anti-Muslim hate and prejudice are often reluctant to share their experiences with the police or another authority. The fact that Islamophobic victimisation is such an under-reported phenomenon (and under-researched topic) suggests that veiled Muslim women often suffer in silence. Increasingly, commentators have begun to differentiate between Islamophobic hostility (that is, hostility directed towards Islam) and anti-Muslim hostility (that is, hostility directed towards Muslim people). Although this issue will be discussed more fully in Chapter 2, it is important to note that we use these terms interchangeably in order to highlight the vulnerability of veiled Muslim women as victims of this type of abuse, particularly since the veil is seen as a symbol of Islam.

Against this background, we examine the lived experiences of Muslim women who wear the veil in public places. In particular, the study investigates the nature of Islamophobic victimisation directed towards veiled Muslim women in public and explores the impact of this victimisation upon veiled Muslim women, their families and wider Muslim communities. Using the English East Midlands city of Leicester as the research case-study area, we employed a variety of methods such as individual and focus group interviews with veiled Muslim women, individual interviews with key stakeholders and policymakers from local organisations, and an ethnographic approach which entailed wearing the veil for prolonged periods of time in different parts of the city. As will be discussed in greater depth in Chapter 3, Leicester was an ideal site in which to conduct this study in light of its religious, cultural and ethnic diversity and large Muslim population.

Chapter 1 examines colonial and popular perceptions of the veil and outlines the significance of this framework for veiled Muslim women. Evidence indicates that in colonial times the veil was seen as a symbol of gender oppression as well as a sign of exoticism. In this sense, the 'liberation' of veiled women became fused with the motivations of imperial expansion. After the terrorist attacks of 9/11 and 7/7, popular stereotypes increasingly portrayed the veil as a symbol of Islamist fundamentalism and self-segregation as well as a sign of gender inequality. The chapter illustrates how the veil has been – and continues to be – perceived as a symbol of Muslim 'otherness' and suggests that its public visibility is key to constructing stereotypes which identify it as a marker of Muslim 'difference'.

DOI: 10.1057/9781137356154.0003

Chapter 2 demonstrates how the aforementioned stereotypes 'legitimise' the acts of violence and hostility directed towards veiled Muslim women when they are seen in public. This chapter defines Islamophobia and interprets Islamophobic victimisation through the lens of gender. From this perspective, gender precipitates manifestations of Islamophobia on the basis that the visibility of the veil, coupled with popular perceptions about veiled Muslim women as oppressed, dangerous and segregated, mark them as 'uniquely' vulnerable to public manifestations of Islamophobia. The gendered dimensions of Islamophobia offer a valuable insight into the process by which veiled Muslim women are identified and subsequently subjected to Islamophobic victimisation in the public sphere.

Chapter 3 presents the methodology used as the basis of our empirical work and outlines the reasoning behind our qualitative approach. It discusses the practicalities of the research methodology, including the processes of developing an interview framework, engaging participants and analysing research material. The chapter also discusses the similarities and differences between the researcher and the researched which are framed by notions of 'insider' and 'outsider' status. As we shall see, being an 'outsider' within the context of research of this nature can benefit the research process by enabling the researcher to elicit in-depth responses whilst at the same time maintaining a critical distance from the interview data.

Chapter 4 reveals the nature of Islamophobic victimisation directed towards veiled Muslim women. It demonstrates that experiences of Islamophobic victimisation – especially 'low-level' types of abuse – are rarely 'one-off' incidents but instead part of a broader continuum of Islamophobia experienced by veiled Muslim women in public places. As a result, this form of victimisation becomes normalised to the extent of being understood as 'ordinary' and 'normal' by veiled Muslim women. Within Chapter 5 we illustrate that both the fear of being attacked and incidents of Islamophobic victimisation can have significant and ongoing consequences for veiled Muslim women, their families and wider Muslim communities. Everyday experiences of both explicit and implicit manifestations of Islamophobia produce, *inter alia*, feelings of inferiority, loss of confidence and self-esteem, depression, flashbacks, guilt and self-blame. Moreover, incidents of Islamophobic victimisation are likely to increase feelings of insecurity, vulnerability and fear amongst veiled Muslim women. Consequently, the threat of Islamophobic victimisation

DOI: 10.1057/9781137356154.0003

limits both the movements and the social interactions of actual and potential victims, thereby resulting in social isolation.

Finally, in Chapter 6 we take stock of the key themes to have emerged from the research findings and offer a more nuanced framework in order to understand the vulnerability of veiled Muslim women as potential victims of anti-Muslim hate and prejudice. This framework recognises the interplay between different aspects of their 'visible' identities and other situational factors. For example, we argue that the vulnerability of veiled Muslim women to Islamophobic attacks in public places depends upon the visibility of their Muslim identity coupled with the visibility of 'other' aspects of their identity alongside factors such as space as well as media reports of local, national and international events related to Islam, Muslims and the veil. Within this framework, we consider what we can do to support them more effectively, and in doing so we make the case for a more nuanced approach to engaging with veiled Muslim women as victims of Islamophobia; one which recognises their multiple vulnerabilities and which takes into consideration their distinct cultural and religious needs.

DOI: 10.1057/9781137356154.0003

1
Constructions of Islam, Gender and the Veil

Abstract: *The chapter examines historical and contemporary discourses of the veil and considers the wider implications of this framework for veiled Muslim women in the West. In colonial times the veil was seen as a symbol of gender oppression in Islam as well as a sign of exoticism. Within this paradigm, the 'liberation' of veiled Muslim women became fused with the motivations of imperial expansion. In a post-9/11 climate, popular perceptions of the veil suggest that it is a symbol of Islamist extremism and segregation as well as a sign of gender inequality. As such, the chapter demonstrates that the veil has been – and continues to be – perceived as a symbol of Muslim 'otherness' and its visibility is key to constructing stereotypes which identify it as a marker of Muslim 'difference'. The chapter then offers a discussion of legal restrictions upon the wearing of the veil in public places in Europe, and argues that perceptions of veiled Muslim women as either oppressed or acting on behalf of a 'terrorist religion' potentially legitimise public acts of violence towards veil wearers. Even if not explicitly inciting hate-motivated violence, popular stereotypes contribute to a climate of intolerance towards veiled Muslim women and to mounting tensions between Islam and the West.*

Zempi, Irene and Neil Chakraborti. *Islamophobia, Victimisation and the Veil.* Basingstoke: Palgrave Macmillan, 2014. DOI: 10.1057/978113735614.0004.

DOI: 10.1057/9781137356154.0004

Orientalism and the veil

Historically and traditionally, Western contact with veiled Muslim women was rare before colonial exploration. Prior to the 17th century, colonial perceptions of veiled Muslim women were the product of male travellers' tales and poor translations of Arabic texts. From the late 17th century, colonial interaction with veiled Muslim women remained limited until the next century when colonial expansion began to produce a 'Western narrative of women in Islam' (Ahmed, 1992: 149). In 1978, Said coined the term 'Orientalism' to portray the way that Western scholarship reflected a distorted image of the East. In particular, the 'Orientalist framework' stemmed from 'an imaginative and yet drastically polarized space dividing the world into two unequal parts, the larger, 'different' one called the Orient, the other, also known as 'our' world, called the Occident or the West' (Said, 1981: 4). This imaginative space was characterised by the strict binary of 'us' and 'them' whereby the West was privileged over the Orient. The ideology associated with Orientalism served to construct a Western identity based on opposition to the Orient. From this perspective, the production of knowledge about the colonial 'Other' was a simultaneous constitution of the 'Self'. This framework was also employed in relation to the dress code of women in Islam.

Within the Orientalist framework, the veiled female body became *the* symbol for Islam. Essentially, the wearing of the veil was seen as evidence of the debasement of women in Islam based on the premise that women were forced to wear the veil by Muslim men. As such, the veil became the symbol of the backwardness of Islam itself. Al-Saji (2010) argues that colonisation functions not only through economic and political hegemony but also by means of a representational apparatus which determines perceptions of the colonised. This apparatus of representation is the lens through which the colonial observer views the colonised society. At the same time though, this lens is also a mirror. The representational apparatus of colonialism not only constitutes the image of the 'native' but posits this image in opposition to a certain self-perception of colonial society. Correspondingly, the veiled female body was projected as the counter image for the ideal Western woman, particularly in the context of gender equality. Against this background, the 'liberation' of veiled Muslim women became the justification for colonialism. During the late 19th and early 20th century colonial officials adopted a 'civilising mission' in relation to colonised countries. The veil took on an acute visibility in

DOI: 10.1057/9781137356154.0004

this attempt, with the image of the subjugated Muslim woman in need of rescue by Western men being used to legitimate the build-up of French and British colonial empires.

At a time when Victorian morals predominated, Muslim women were the objects of male erotic fantasies related to the idea of harem.[1] An eroticised desire to remove the veil was evident in the growing European print culture of the 18th century. Mabro's (1991) study of Western travellers' perceptions of Middle Eastern women found that they were seen as 'exotic' and the veil was placed at the centre of this exoticism. For Mabro (1991), a desire to 'uncover what was covered' and to 'see the unseen' was a constant feature within colonial discourses, thus pointing to a libidinal desire to unveil the veiled female body. The same image was evident in Orientalist paintings in which Middle Eastern women were frequently portrayed naked or scantily clad lounging in harems (Haddad, 2007). However, it was also argued that these women were unhappy in their harem and thus in need of rescue by the West. Vulnerable, naked women who needed to be rescued by Western men were presented as the victims of cruel Eastern men. It is this image of captive beauty that appealed to the patriarchal urges of domination and imperialism of Western men. Clearly, such paintings presented a sharp contrast between the barbarity of the East and the civility of the West, between 'us' and 'them'.

Western men were prohibited from entering the private world, including harems, where unveiled women could be viewed, and as a result the removal of the veil signified the ultimate form of colonisation. In this regard, the objectification of the veil as a form of visibility of sexual desire to unveil the veiled female body became fused with the motivations of imperial expansion. The visible transformation from veiled bodies to 'Westernised' bodies was a key factor in subduing resistance towards colonial powers through imposing 'Western values' upon them. Billaud and Castro (2013) observe that the removal of all distinctive signs, and especially the veil, from the public domain was key to the assimilation of the colonised. Ultimately, removing women's veils became a central motive of the so-called civilising mission on the basis that the veil was seen as a visible barrier to the establishment of Western superiority.

In colonial times, therefore, the veil was invested with a twofold visibility of desire: a sexual desire to see beneath the veil in parallel with a desire to 'civilise' and 'modernise' Middle Eastern women by removing their veils. From this perspective, the veil was seen as a symbol of gender

DOI: 10.1057/9781137356154.0004

oppression in Islam as well as a sign of exoticism, whilst the 'liberation' of veiled women became fused with the motivations of imperial expansion, at least from the gaze of the coloniser. This approach of viewing veiled women as subjects who can and should be unveiled functions as a contemporary precedent for the state's desire to remove the veil in public places and to 'see the unseen'. This indicates that colonial ways of seeing the veil still function as a lens through which to view veiled Muslim women, particularly in certain European countries such as France, Belgium and Italy where the wearing of the veil has been banned in public.

Contemporary understandings of the veil

In colonial times the image of the subjugated veiled Muslim woman in need of rescue by Western men dominated the gaze of the colonisers. In a post-9/11 climate, popular perceptions of the veil suggest that it is a symbol of Islamist extremism and self-segregation as well as a sign of gender oppression. Such negative connotations of the veil interact with each other whilst promoting the veil as a 'threat' in the West. Although there is an overlap amongst these misconceptions of the veil it is necessary to assess them separately, particularly since they promote Islamophobia in different ways. As the following discussion demonstrates, the wearing of the veil in the West attracts negative attention premised on three main arguments: gender equality, public safety and integration.

Gender oppression

The wearing of the veil in public places in the West is routinely perceived as a marker of patriarchy and a symbol of gender subjugation. From this perspective, the female code of dress in Islam functions as a metonym for the perceived backwardness of Islam. The assumption of patriarchal domination and matriarchal submissiveness in Islam consolidates and reproduces oriental views of Islam as culturally inferior to the West. Based on the rigid dichotomy of 'us' and 'them', the act of veiling is constructed as evidence of the misogyny and violence associated with Islam whilst the act of unveiling is identified as an example of the equa-

DOI: 10.1057/9781137356154.0004

tion of the West with gender equality and freedom. Accordingly, the veil is stereotypically seen as a symbol for the oppression of women against which the West prides itself as being emancipator.

Within this paradigm, popular stereotypes about women in Islam provide the negative mirror in which Western constructions of gender can be positively reflected. By erasing the multiplicity and variety of veiled Muslim women's lived experiences, they are constructed as 'Other' compared to the emancipated Western women. In striking contrast to the image of the oppressed veiled Muslim woman stands the image of the emancipated Western (and non-Muslim) woman who has 'control over her income, her body and her sexuality' (Kapur, 2002: 16). From this perspective, the reduction of images of Muslim women to monolithic categories maintains the construction of the Muslim as 'Other' whereby Muslim women are underprivileged and oppressed, 'with the West being the primary referent in theory and praxis' (Raju, 2002: 173).

Critique of veiling practices located on the 'us' and 'them' dichotomy infers that the increasing visibility of veiled female bodies in the public sphere is indicative of 'Muslimness' rather than femininity. This approach is based on a simplistic equation between sexual expressiveness and bodily display. As Macdonald (2006) points out, Western imagination is itself obsessed with bodies and the possibility of revealing the female body. Popular images of women in the media promote a 'natural', 'open' and 'unveiled' female body which is constructed through regimes of internalised management such as diet, exercise and even plastic surgery, whilst promoting the open visibility of glamorous, white, youthful, female bodies. In striking contrast to this image stands the image of the veiled Muslim woman who is perceived to be sexually constrained, illiterate, tradition-bound, domesticated and poor. In the words of Kapur (2002: 18), 'it is an image that is strikingly reminiscent of the colonial construction of the Eastern woman'. This approach is structured along the contours of colonial reasoning: the assumption being that women in Islam are incapable of self-determination and autonomy. Seen in this light, a body that is veiled is necessarily a victimised body to the extent that veiled Muslim women are incapable of autonomy or agency.

In concretising the symbolism of the veil as a form of gender oppression, anti-veiling discourse denies the voices of veiled Muslim women while professing a desire for their voices to be heard. Although the veil debate revolves around the right to freedom of speech and expression, the individuals are not heard, and mute symbols are often presented as

DOI: 10.1057/9781137356154.0004

'clear' and in no need of interpretation or explanation. Consequently, the multiple meanings of the veil are taken to be self-evident, as representing the subordination of women in Islam, whilst the voices of the Muslim women who choose to veil are almost entirely missing from the public sphere. Ultimately, the veil as an expression of religion, a sign of personal autonomy and a display of freedom of expression is ignored. Without dismissing the fact that some women, Muslim or not, are oppressed by men and by customs, this is not the appropriate framework in which to explore veiling, particularly in liberal democratic states such as the UK.

On the one hand, women in certain Muslim countries such as Saudi Arabia are forced to wear the veil and this can be a very traumatic experience. On the other hand, veiling in a liberal democratic country such as the UK (where veiling is voluntary) indicates that it is a choice, particularly as a symbol of Muslim identity. Indeed, the research literature suggests that the veil represents freedom of choice within the UK (Bullock, 2011; Hannan, 2011; Mondal, 2008; Tarlo, 2007; Franks, 2000). Echoing the same view, Ferrari (2013) states that interpreting the veil exclusively as a marker of gender oppression neglects the fact that there are women who choose to wear the veil. However, Billaud and Castro (2013) claim that the apparently autonomous decision to wear the veil is the result of a false consciousness rather than a genuine choice. This would suggest that veiled Muslim women are not simply oppressed but also 'blind' to their own oppression.

The failure to acknowledge the possibility of the autonomy of veiled Muslim women and girls ensures the continued representation of women in Islam as 'voiceless victims'. Moreover, dominant perceptions about veiled Muslim women's lack of agency further entrench dangerous notions of a 'Muslim problem' whereby Muslim men deny Muslim women the freedom to exercise their autonomy. As Ahmad (2010) notes, this discourse silences and obscures alternative forms of agency, repeats simplistic 'Western' versus 'Muslim' dichotomous frameworks, and contributes to the separation between 'us' and 'them'. While we acknowledge that the social status and life conditions of many Muslim women needs to be improved to achieve gender equality, it should also be recognised that to consider all Muslim women as passive victims is not an accurate reflection of how many Muslim women perceive their lives. Ultimately, the articulation of the female Muslim body as the 'victim subject' fails to accommodate a multi-layered experience and therefore denies the possibility of choice.

DOI: 10.1057/9781137356154.0004

Islamist terrorism

The wearing of the veil in public places in the West is stereotypically seen as a symbol of Islamist fundamentalism. In a post-9/11 climate, the West is allegedly facing a global 'threat' by Islamist extremism and the veil is a visual reprocentation of that 'threat'. Ghumman and Ryan (2013) argue that although Muslim women are perceived as oppressed and Muslim men are seen as dangerous, Muslim women are not free from popular stereotypes whereby Muslims *per se* are seen as terrorists or terrorist sympathisers. In particular, the veil is perceived as a danger to public safety on the basis that the covering of the face hinders identification. An example of the link between the veil and Islamist terrorism is evident in several high profile cases in the UK and elsewhere. In December 2006, Mustaf Jama, a Somali asylum seeker wanted for the murder of a British female police officer, fled the UK dressed as a woman dressed in burka and using his sister's passport, despite being amongst the UK's most wanted criminals at the time and Heathrow airport being in a state of alert following the 7/7 bombings (Stokes, 2006). Moreover, one of the terrorists responsible for the 7/7 bombings had allegedly fled London disguised in burka (BBC News, 2007). In November 2013, terror suspect Mohammed Ahmed Mohammed escaped surveillance in London by entering a mosque wearing Western clothes, but leaving the mosque disguised as a veiled woman (*The Guardian*, 2013a).

Correspondingly, the veil is stereotypically seen as a danger to public safety on the basis that it could be used as camouflage for a terrorist. In this light, banning the veil is seen as a means to ensure public safety. It is important to note that there is no veil ban in the UK but schools and educational institutions are allowed to set their own uniform guidelines. In 2005, Imperial College in London banned its students from wearing the veil on campus over security concerns raised by the terrorist attacks of 7/7 (Garner, 2005). In 2006, Birmingham University School of Medicine banned its medical students from wearing the veil when talking to patients in hospitals and surgeries, and when they were in meetings with other medical staff (Leggatt, Dixon and Milland, 2006). In September 2013 Birmingham Metropolitan College banned its students from wearing the veil on campus so that they were easily identifiable. The UK Prime Minister, David Cameron, supported this decision but the Deputy Prime Minister, Nick Clegg, stated that he was uneasy about the veil ban (BBC News, 2013). In 2010, Damian Green,

DOI: 10.1057/9781137356154.0004

then immigration minister, had stated that banning the wearing of the veil in public would be 'un-British' (BBC News, 2010). Birmingham Metropolitan College has later reversed its decision after more than 9,000 people signed an online petition set up by the National Union of Students (NUS) Black Students' Campaign calling on the College to remove the ban (*The Guardian*, 2013b).

As a sign of Islamist terrorism and extremism, the veil is also understood as a tool of religious fundamentalism whereby it serves to proselytise non-Muslims to Islam. In this regard, the veil is seen as an act of religious propaganda with the aim to infiltrate into Western society. In the words of Tissot (2011: 43): 'Women in niqab are the Trojan horse of extremist Islamism'. Seen in this light, the veil hides not only the face but 'secret intentions' as well, namely, to impose Sharia law in the West. As such, the veil represents the type of political Islamism that is also found in Iraq and Afganistan, characterising the implementation of Sharia law as interpreted by the Taliban. From this perspective, Muslim girls and women who veil in the UK are often linked to political Islam.

In 2002 Shabina Begum, aged 15 at the time, pursued a legal case against Denbigh High School in Luton on the grounds that it had unlawfully denied her the 'right to education and to manifest her religious beliefs' for its ban on the jilbab, a traditional Islamic dress that leaves only the hands and face exposed (Johnston, 2005). The then head teacher at Denbigh High School in Luton stated that the school maintained its jilbab ban to help students to resist the efforts of extremist Muslim groups to recruit them (Johnston, 2005). It was believed that after her parents died, Begum came under influence of her brother, a supporter of the Islamic political party, Hizb ut-Tahrir. For Hizb ut-Tahrir and its members, the Muslim dress is a flag for Islam, designed not only to display the Muslim woman's rejection of Western capitalism, secularism and integration, but also to draw infidels towards submission to Allah (Tarlo, 2007). The High Court dismissed Begum's application for judicial review, ruling she had failed to show that the school, where 79 per cent of pupils were Muslim, had either excluded her or breached her human rights (Halpin, 2005). This was overturned by the Court of Appeal, which stated that the school had unlawfully excluded Begum, denied her the right to manifest her religion, and denied her access to suitable and appropriate education (Johnston, 2005).

DOI: 10.1057/9781137356154.0004

At the stroke of a pen, schoolgirls who veil are linked to Islamist terror-ism and the subjugation of women in Islam. Embedded in such statements is the underlying assumption that Muslim girls and women who veil do so from within frameworks of coercive constraint. As Fernandez (2009) observes, one of the key concerns in the Begum case was whether the applicant's decision to wear the jilbab was made entirely freely or whether she had been subjected to pressure from her brother. Such assumptions of a coercive element ignore the possibility of free choice whilst, at the same time, denying the possibility of a legal framework that promotes a permis-sive understanding of adolescent autonomy. Equally importantly, as Malik points out (2008: 99), one must guard against 'the dangers of conflating religious differences with national security risks'. The fact that the wearing of the veil might be used by certain individuals to commit crime or even acts for the purposes of terrorism is not a legitimate reason for banning it. In short, legislation which bans the wearing of the veil constitutes a human rights violation and also undercuts individual agency, privacy and self-expression no less than in countries where women are forced to veil. This point is explored further in due course.

National cohesion

The wearing of the veil in public places in the West is routinely under-stood as a marker of segregation. Seen in this light, the wearing of the veil hinders full integration and fosters the social isolation of veiled Muslim women. Moreover, it mirrors the notion of 'parallel lives' and self-enclosed communities. From this perspective, multiculturalism is seen as a 'threat' to the existence of Western values, and the veil – by virtue of its public visibility as *the* sign of Islam in the West – is a visual symbol of that 'threat'. In the British context, national identity and examples of Muslim 'difference' are cast as mutually exclusive. As such, the veil is rejected on the grounds that it is non-British in inception and adoption, thereby erasing the principle of integration as a two-way proc-ess of mutual accommodation by all; rather, it is integration at the price of becoming less 'Muslim' (Meer, Dwyer and Modood, 2010). Thus, the argument goes, veiled Muslim women must unveil themselves in order to integrate into Western society.

The rhetoric of the veil as a 'statement of separation and of difference',[2] was maintained by Kettle (2006) who stated that it is 'not merely a badge of religious or cultural identity like a turban, a yarmulke or even a baseball

DOI: 10.1057/9781137356154.0004

cap'; rather, it indicates rejection. In this sense, the veil is seen as 'different' to other forms of religious attire – including Muslim. Rather, the wearing of the veil signals a visibility that is 'conspicuous' in comparison to other religious signs, which themselves do not attract public attention and, though also visible, remain 'normalised'. As such, the veil is 'unique' on the basis that it prevents a basic form of human contact in a way that the Muslim headscarf, the Sikh turban, the Buddhist robe or the Christian Cross do not. Contrary to other examples of religious attire which allow for the face to be visible, the veil cancels the wearer's identity. According to this line of argument, the veil relegates the wearer to a condition of isolation and segregation due to the difficulty in communicating with a person whose face is covered. From this perspective, the veil is seen as hindrance to direct communication because it allegedly makes inter-personal communication less open and transparent. Correspondingly, Robert (2005: 28) states:

> It is as if, once you put on the niqab you cease to have a human identity. I know that the niqab is a shock to the system for most people in non-Muslim societies – we are used to seeing so much personal information about people around us, being able to tell their race, their age, their physique and their attractiveness. The niqab gives none of this information.

Echoing the same view, Mancini (2013: 27) argues that a covered face cancels transparency and reciprocity in communication, highlighting 'the objective and undeniable difficulty of communication that derives from the almost total covering of a woman's face'. In this context, transparency and reciprocity is impeded by the covering of the face. Along similar lines, Tourkochoriti (2012: 845) observes that in Christianity the face has become the 'quintessence of the person', the 'noble part of the body', whilst the covering of the face marks an 'undignified' existence. From this perspective, the veil is contrary to Christian/Western civilisation, which values the face and in which interactions among citizens are necessarily unveiled.

This discussion shows that the wearing of the veil is routinely seen as an obstacle to face-to-face interaction, and consequently as a sign of isolation and self-segregation. It would appear, then, that the community cohesion agenda is based exclusively upon the obligation of Muslim minorities to integrate, and as a result the problem of non-integration rests with Muslims themselves (Meer et al., 2010). The concept of integration does not allow for 'difference' in general and 'Muslim distinctiveness' in particular; rather, 'real' integration can only be achieved through greater public conformity, in sharp contrast to a multicultural

DOI: 10.1057/9781137356154.0004

integration that sustains 'difference'. According to this line of argument, the removal of the veil is an essential step to community cohesion on the basis that the covering of the face is a visible barrier to community relations. Indeed, the practice of veiling has acquired huge significance in the discourse on Muslim integration. Muslim women are viewed as the main vehicles of integration but simultaneously they are the first victims of the failure of integration. Ironically, choosing to veil is a greater offence than being forced to veil, or as Khiabany and Williamson (2008: 69) put it: 'Veiled women are considered to be ungrateful subjects who have failed to assimilate and are deemed to threaten the British way of life'. Even in cases where women choose to wear the veil, they are seen as deliberately isolating themselves and rejecting Western values. Ultimately, the parameters of the veil debate demonstrate that multiculturalism is an implicit expression of the degree of tolerance of the 'host' state that demands the integration of the Muslim 'Other' on its own terms. Within this framework, the visibility of the veil in the West is key to constructing popular stereotypes of the veil as a marker of Muslim 'difference'.

The visibility of the veil

The veil does not attract public attention in an Islamic state where the majority of women wear it but it does attract attention in countries when veiling is a rare practice. Ferrari (2013) acknowledges that wearing the veil in public places in the West attracts attention instead of passing 'unobserved'. In this case, the veil monopolises the image of Islam, whilst hiding the very existence of Muslim women not wearing it. From this perspective, the visibility and invisibility of the female Muslim body becomes central in promoting the veil as a symbol of Muslim 'otherness'.

Western discourses require female sexual agency and desire to be inscribed in the openness to view the female body. Thus, the argument goes, the more 'liberated' a woman, the more 'civilised' the society. Although it regards itself as liberal, the West requires women to have particular experiences and to define themselves in certain ways; rather, 'most of all it requires that women be the object of the gaze' (Franks, 2000: 927). This argument draws its concept of the 'gaze' from the panoptic gaze that Foucault describes in *Discipline and Punish* (1977). This point is crucial to understanding the concept of visibility in the discussion

DOI: 10.1057/9781137356154.0004

of the veil. Franks (2000) presents a development of this line of argument which recognises that there is a hierarchy of gazes that changes according to location. Within this paradigm, the Muslim woman who veils becomes the object of the gaze in a non-Muslim milieu such as the UK. In this context, the praxis of veiling in the UK has the 'unintended consequence' of attracting the non-Muslim gaze. This emphasises the 'difference' between the veiled and the non-veiled female body.

Essentialised perceptions of veiled Muslim women as docile, oppressed and 'hidden' behind their veils are products of a colonial mode of construction and representation. This phallocentric gaze – or to use Frye's (1983) term 'arrogant vision' – sees the female body as an object of male desire whilst defining her subject-position through that gaze. Representations of veiled Muslim women as symbols of gender oppression are generated by such vision, specifically by a gaze that 'wants to see'. As Al-Saji (2010) points out, vision is not a mere neutral recording of the visible. In Foucault's terms, the concept of the 'object of the gaze' operates upon the assumption of an 'ideal' spectator. This approach promotes a particular way of seeing and of being seen. Foucault's theoretical framework ascribes control over the gaze to the 'ideal spectator' to critique the images created through that gaze. Under this idea, the veil constitutes a form of visibility of desire; a desire to remove the veil and view the unseen. For Yegenoglu (1998: 12), the desire to penetrate behind the veil is 'characterised by a desire to master, control, and reshape the body of the subjects by making them visible'. The veil with its rich connotations marks the foe, whilst the aim of unveiling the veiled female Muslim body provides justification for radical action (Klaus and Kassel, 2005). Respectively, the veil constitutes an obstacle to desire to see behind the veil and as a result an object of frustration and aggressiveness. Following this line of thought, Muslim women may be targeted because they 'stand out' from accepted norms, and as a result fail to conform to society's expectations of sexual behaviour and gender performance. Ultimately, the symbol of the unveiled female Muslim body becomes a sign of victory.

Within the framework of a theory of the gaze the options of resistance left to the objectified are constructed within a binary opposition. This means that veiled Muslim women resist the gaze by remaining veiled or relent to the gaze by unveiling. The former correlates with the view that the veil is read as a marker of resistance to Western identity. Indeed, the concept of the visible portrays the veil as a nexus

DOI: 10.1057/9781137356154.0004

of competing national images and identities. Under this interpretation, the physical appearance of the veiled body seems challenging or intimidating to both Western, non-Muslim viewers and 'Westernised' Muslim viewers. In particular, the presence of veiled Muslim women may be perceived as 'threatening', especially to those viewers who are convinced that Muslims are a 'threat' *per se*. Consequently, veiled Muslim women may be 'punished' for their supposedly deviant identity performance by being attacked verbally and physically in the public domain of the street. In the eyes of the attacker, veiled Muslim women are 'taught a lesson' about what happens when they do not conform by removing the veil in public places in the West. Relatedly, certain European countries have applied restrictive measures and bans on the visibility of the veil in the public sphere thereby criminalising the veil and those Muslim women who continue to wear it.

The criminalisation of the veil

The preceding discussion illustrates popular stereotypes of the veil as a visible marker of gender oppression, Islamist terrorism and self-segregation. In light of this, the practice of veiling represents an unacceptable 'otherness', an unwelcome religious, cultural and racial presence (Grillo and Shah, 2013). The ubiquitous assumption that the veil accentuates Muslim 'Otherness' *vis-à-vis* Western values paints the veil as 'dangerous' whilst ignoring its multi-layered symbolism. Despite its multiple levels of meaning as a sign of religious and personal freedom, popular understandings of the veil indicate that veiled Muslim women are either oppressed or acting on behalf of a 'terrorist religion'. Correspondingly, several European countries have enforced legislation which makes it illegal for Muslim women to wear the veil in public. In 2011, France became the first country in Europe to introduce a law banning the wearing of the veil in public places.[3] Relatedly, it is important to note that in 2004 France enacted a law banning the hijab for students in public schools.[4] In particular, the legislation prohibited the display of 'conspicuous' religious symbols such as the Jewish skullcap, the Christian crucifix and the Sikh turban by the students of public elementary and high schools. According to Lyon and Spini (2004), this law appeared to deal with religious symbols *per se*, although the public debate was mostly concerned with the Muslim headscarf.

DOI: 10.1057/9781137356154.0004

Belgium was the second European country after France to enforce a veil ban. Following the example set by France and Belgium, the Dutch government has agreed to introduce a ban on face covering in public. In Italy, a parliamentary commission has approved a draft law banning women from wearing veils in public whilst an old anti-terrorist law against concealing the face for security reasons has already been used by some local Italian authorities to fine Muslim women who wear the veil. In Spain, the city of Barcelona has announced a veil ban in some public spaces such as municipal offices, public markets and libraries, whilst at least two smaller towns in Catalonia have already imposed veil bans. Grillo and Shah (2013) point out that while local in origin, moves to ban the veil are usually followed by other countries. As such, there exists a cross-national interweaving of media, political and public discourses against the Islamisation of Europe and in favour of restrictions on the practice of Islam in the West. The Council of Europe Parliamentary Assembly (2010) legitimises the veil ban on the basis that the wearing of the veil is seen as a 'threat' to gender equality, public safety and national cohesion.

> The veiling of women, especially full veiling through the burqa or the niqab, is often perceived as a symbol of the subjugation of women to men, restricting the role of women within society, limiting their professional life and impeding their social and economic activities ... Article 9 of the Convention includes the right of individuals to choose freely to wear or not to wear religious clothing in private or in public. Legal restrictions to this freedom may be justified where necessary in a democratic society, in particular for security purposes or where public or professional functions of individuals require their religious neutrality or that their face can be seen.

Although it acknowledges that Muslim women have the right to freedom of religious expression, the Council of Europe justifies the implementation of legal restrictions upon the wearing of the veil in public in Europe. Correspondingly, justifications in favour of the veil ban in public in European countries generally take three forms: covering the face is incompatible with Western values including gender equality; wearing the veil impedes communication and integration; and wearing the veil poses a security risk. The British government has not entertained a veil ban so far. In this regard, there are no legislative or administrative provisions which forbid the wearing of the veil at the national or local level. Contrary to France, the UK does not have a tradition of *laïcité* and enforced secularism; rather, its patrimony lies in an established state church which affords liberal tolerance to those of all religious persuasions or none (Hill, 2013).

DOI: 10.1057/9781137356154.0004

However, although the UK does not have any legislative prohibitions in place, there are calls for such legislation to be introduced. In 2010, the Conservative MP Philip Hollobone sought to introduce a Private Members' Bill, entitled 'The Face Coverings Regulations Bill', which would make it illegal for people to cover their faces in public. The Bill, which received its second reading in the House of Commons in December 2011, was rejected. The British National Party and the UK Independence Party both supported a veil ban in their election manifestos in 2010 whilst extreme protest movements such as the English Defence League have staged a number of violent anti-Muslim protests against elements of Islam such as Sharia law, mosques and the veil.

Although there is no official policy on the Muslim code of dress in the UK, there has been considerable debate. After Birmingham Metropolitan College dropped a ban on students wearing veils, the Home Office minister Jeremy Browne stated that the government should consider banning Muslim girls from wearing veils in public places, and urged for a national debate to take place (BBC News, 2013). In a similar vein, Conservative MP Sarah Wollaston stated that the veil makes its wearers 'invisible' and prevents some women from 'participating fully and equally in society' (BBC News, 2013). A 2013 poll by Channel 4 News showed that 55 per cent of the public supported a veil ban in all public places whilst 81 per cent supported a veil ban in schools, courts and hospitals. Additionally, two YouGov[5] polls from the same year showed strong levels of opposition towards the niqab, although more tolerance of the hijab as a more 'acceptable' form of Muslim dress in comparison to the niqab.

Against this background, the context in which the debate about the 'appropriateness' of the veil takes place, within the UK and elsewhere, tends to be that of Huntington's thesis of civilisational clash. Within this paradigm, the figure of the veiled female Muslim body becomes a central point in the battle between the West and the Muslim 'Other', whilst defying the specificities of the lived experiences of veiled Muslim women. By the veiling and unveiling of Muslim women, Islam is illustrated, interpreted and marked as a completely 'different' world whereby the veil signifies the border between Islam and the West. Contemporary stereotypes of the veil play a central role in this imaginary construct, 'underwriting the binary of freedom and oppression and the modes of gender and subjectivity through which the "West" maintains its imaginary borders' (Al-Saji, 2010: 878).

DOI: 10.1057/9781137356154.0004

Along similar lines, Tourkochoriti (2012) points out that the veil ban, like the hijab ban in public schools in France, is justified by the need to protect Muslim girls and women from being forced to wear it by their families or local community. It also aims to protect them from themselves when wearing the veil happens to be an authentic choice of the women concerned. In this regard, Muslim women are denied the possibility to be active agents capable of rational choices, as they are considered to be alienated and 'blind' to their own oppression. Although religions in general may provide the means and justification for the subjection of women, a distorted view of Islam denies recognition of women's autonomy in Islam.

Clearly, the veil debate has not translated into a sophisticated under-standing of the ways in which veiled Muslim women's lives and experi-ences are mediated by factors such as gender, age, religion, ethnicity, race, class and space, to name a few. Rather, the gradual mutation of the veil from a symbol of religious identity to a contentious marker of 'differ-ence' paves the way for further contamination of the veil as a visible sign of Muslim 'otherness'. Ultimately, the veil ban – including support for state veil bans – prevents veiled Muslim women from full participation in society by exacerbating their multiple and intersectional discrimina-tion on the grounds of both religion and gender, thereby increasing (rather than decreasing) social exclusion by pushing these women to the margins of society (see also Chakraborti and Zempi, 2013).

The law also stigmatises veiled Muslim women as 'criminals', thereby potentially 'legitimising' acts of violence towards them when they are seen in public. In this sense, the veil ban increases the sense of vulner-ability of Muslim women dressed in niqab in the public sphere. Even if not explicitly inciting hate-motivated violence, the law in its application contributes to a climate of intolerance and to mounting tensions between Islam and the West. As Ferrari (2013) points out, criminal law is not the best instrument for dealing with the problems raised by covering one's face; rather, in a genuinely liberal society criminal law should be the last resort for when it is not possible to protect people's rights. Under this idea, other instruments such as education, debate and persuasion should be implemented to promote an open discussion within the Muslim community on the role of the veil in the public sphere in the West and elsewhere.

In conclusion, it is clear that the veil has become an important symbol in the homogenisation and demonisation of Islam and Muslims. This has

DOI: 10.1057/9781137356154.0004

become all the more evident in the context of intense political, media and public scrutiny over the visibility of Islam in the West in relation to broader concerns about issues of integration and terrorism. Against this background, the veil finds itself confined within discourses of 'difference' and 'otherness'. This chapter has explored popular perceptions of the veil as a symbol of gender oppression, Islamist terrorism and a 'threat' to Western values, and evidence suggests that the significance of veiling practices is often ignored. In this regard, both historical and contemporary constructions of the veil ignore the specificities of veiled women's lived experiences. Moreover, perceptions of veiled Muslim women as either oppressed or acting on behalf of a 'terrorist religion' potentially legitimise acts of violence towards veiled Muslim women when they are seen in public. Correspondingly, moves to restrict the wearing of the veil in public places do little more than legitimise the acts of violence and hostility directed towards veiled Muslim women.

Notes

1   The harem was the space in which veiled Muslim women could be uncovered.
2   In 2006 the comments of Jack Straw, then British Home Secretary, attracted considerable publicity when he stated that the veil is a 'visible statement of separation and of difference', and that it can weaken community relations.
3   French law number 2010–1192 of 11 October 2010.
4   French law number 2004–228 of 15 March 2004.
5   YouGov is a research company which is based in the UK.

DOI: 10.1057/9781137356154.0004

2
Unveiling Islamophobic Victimisation

Abstract: *The chapter examines the nature and extent of Islamophobic victimisation. It also explores explanations behind this type of victimisation through the lens of gender. Evidence suggests that veiled Muslim women are at heightened risk of Islamophobic victimisation by virtue of their visible 'Muslimness'. Popular perceptions that veiled Muslim women are passive, oppressed and powerless increase their chance of assault, thereby marking them as 'easy' targets to attack. Furthermore, attacks towards veiled Muslim women are justified because of the conflation of Islam with terrorism. Collectively, these arguments highlight the gendered dimensions of Islamophobic victimisation. The chapter emphasises that there is no single monolithic Muslim experience of Islamophobia. Recognising the interplay of different aspects of victims' identities with other personal, social and situational factors is highly relevant to understanding the vulnerability of veiled Muslim women as victims of Islamophobia.*

Zempi, Irene and Neil Chakraborti. *Islamophobia, Victimisation and the Veil.* Basingstoke: Palgrave Macmillan, 2014. DOI: 10.1057/978113735614.0005.

Conceptualising Islamophobia

In the current climate, Islam and Muslims find themselves under siege. The Orientalist roots of the process of 'Othering' of Islam and Muslims paved the way for the current climate of Islamophobia, although the 9/11 and subsequent terrorist attacks have played a major role in heightening Islamophobic perceptions of Muslims in the West. In other words, contemporary Islamophobia is a reflection of a historical anti-Muslim, anti-Islamic phenomenon which was constructed in colonial times but which has increased significantly in recent times, creating a deeper resentment and fear of Islam and of Muslims than existed before. Seen through the prism of security risk, incompatible difference and self-segregation, Muslims in the West have emerged as the new 'folk devils' of popular and media imagination. Within this paradigm, Islam is understood as a violent political ideology, religion and culture; Muslim men are perceived as the embodiment of terrorism, fundamentalism and extremism; and Muslim women are viewed as the personification of gender oppression in Islam, especially if they are veiled. Ultimately, such stereotypes provide fertile ground for public expressions of Islamophobia including verbal abuse, threats and intimidation, harassment, physical assault and violence, property damage, hate mail and literature, as well as offensive online and internet abuse.

For the purposes of this discussion, it is important to differentiate between the terms 'Islamophobia' and 'Islamophobic victimisation'. According to Mythen, Walklate and Khan (2009), the concept of 'victimisation' is understood as the act by which someone is rendered a victim, the experience of being a victim in parallel with the socio-cultural process by which this occurs. This conceptual framework indicates that victimisation can be 'ideological' (for example pertaining to ideas and concepts that victimise individuals or groups) or it can have material consequences for those who are victimised (for example through verbal and physical abuse). From this perspective, it could be argued that the concept of Islamophobia is 'ideological' as it refers to an abstract notion of antipathy to Islam whilst the notion of Islamophobic victimisation refers to the material dimensions of this anti-Islamic, anti-Muslim hostility. Under this interpretation, Islamophobic victimisation refers to manifestations of Islamophobia on the basis that it is the acting out of that antipathy.

DOI: 10.1057/9781137356154.0005

In 1997, the publication of the Runnymede Trust report entitled *Islamophobia: A Challenge for Us All* was the first report to raise awareness about the problem of Islamophobia in the UK and elsewhere. It defined Islamophobia as 'the shorthand way of referring to dread or hatred of Islam – and, therefore, to fear or dislike all or most Muslims' (Runnymede Trust, 1997: 1). Building upon this definition, we have described Islamophobia as "a fear or hatred of Islam that translates into ideological and material forms of cultural racism against obvious markers of 'Muslimness'" (Chakraborti and Zempi, 2012: 271). Using this framework we emphasise the link between the ideology of Islamophobia and manifestations of such attitudes, triggered by the visibility of the victim's (perceived) Muslim identity. This approach interprets Islamophobia as a 'new' form of racism, whereby Islamic religion, tradition and culture are seen as a 'threat' to the Western way of life.

It is important to recognise that racism can occur in situations where neither the reality nor concept of race actually exists. As Meer et al. (2010) point out, understandings of racism should not focus exclusively on race thereby overlooking religion and culture. According to this line of argument, conceptualising racism exclusively as a form of 'biological determinism' ignores the ways in which cultural racism draws upon other markers of 'difference' to identify minority groups and individuals that do not conform with mainstream society. Modood (1997: 165) explains that:

> Cultural racism is likely to be particularly aggressive against those minority communities that want to maintain – and not just defensively – some of the basic elements of their culture or religion; if, far from denying their difference (beyond the colour of their skin), they want to assert this difference in public, and demand that they be respected just as they are.

Taking a similar position, Law (2010) highlights the complex chameleon-like character of racism, which changes in terms of form and content across different times and contexts. For Zebiri (2008), colour racism has ceased to be 'acceptable'; nevertheless, a cultural racism which emphasises the 'other', alien values of Muslims has increased, especially in light of popular debates of national identity, immigration and community cohesion. For advocates of the 'clash of civilisations' thesis, there is a cultural war between Islam and the West. In the British context, Islam and Muslims have increasingly been seen to be 'culturally dangerous' and threatening 'the British way of life'. Whilst recognising that Muslim

DOI: 10.1057/9781137356154.0005

minorities differ in the context of European countries – predominantly Algerian in France, Turkish in Germany and Austria, Pakistani in the UK – it is increasingly Islamic religion, tradition and culture that have been seen as a 'threat' to the Western ideals of democracy, freedom of speech and gender equality. At the same time though, it is often argued that Islamophobia 'does not exist'. For example, atheist Richard Dawkins stated that racism against a religion cannot exist on the basis that 'It is not a race ... Islam is a religion', whilst British journalist Andrew Gilligan stated that anti-Muslim hate crime has been exaggerated by 'the Islamo-phobia industry' (Shackle, 2013). Our previous work has acknowledged that the prevalence of Islamophobic victimisation is difficult to measure, as it is both an under-researched topic and under-reported phenomenon (Chakraborti and Zempi, 2012). Nevertheless, existing evidence lends weight to the view that Islamophobia does exist, as can be seen in the following analysis of the existing literature.

Nature of Islamophobic victimisation

In their ground-breaking report, *Islamophobia: A Challenge for Us All*, the Runnymede Trust (1997) examined the extent and forms of anti-Muslim hostility and prejudice in Britain. It was established that Islamophobic attitudes had become 'more explicit, more extreme and more danger-ous ... prevalent in all sections of society' (Runnymede Trust, 1997: 1). The report also noted how Islamophobia was becoming a 'fact of life' for many British Muslim women. Focusing on Islamophobia in the Euro-pean Union (EU) following 9/11, Allen and Nielsen (2002) found that typical manifestations of Islamophobia included incidents of verbal and physical abuse targeted towards Muslim women. In particular, Muslim women who wore the hijab were the most likely targets for verbal abuse, being spat upon, having their headscarves torn from them and being physically assaulted. Mosques were also attacked, ranging from minor vandalism to arson and firebombs.

Moreover, the Home Office (2001) report *Religious Discrimination in England and Wales* noted that for the majority of Muslim respondents verbal abuse and hostility had become commonplace, especially post-9/11. Along similar lines, McGhee (2005) observed that there was a four-fold increase in the number of racist attacks reported by British Muslims and other Asian, ostensibly 'Muslim-looking', groups in the UK during

DOI: 10.1057/9781137356154.0005

the months immediately after 9/11. This heightened sense of vulnerability since 9/11 has also been reported in Garland and Chakraborti's (2004) studies of racism in rural England. In the three weeks following the 7/7 bombings, police figures showed a six-fold increase in the number of religiously motivated offences reported in London, the vast majority of which were directed against Muslim households and places of worship, whilst in the same three-week period over 1,200 suspected Islamophobic incidents were recorded by police force across the UK (BBC News, 2005).

Similar findings were evident in the report *Islamophobia: Issues, Challenges and Action* published by the Commission on British Muslims and Islamophobia (2004). The Commission emphasised the high levels of anti-Muslim hostility targeted towards Muslims. It also highlighted the vulnerability of Muslim women wearing hijabs as victims of Islamophobia. In a similar vein, the report *Muslims in the UK: Policies for Engaged Citizens* highlighted that post-9/11 Muslim women had suffered high levels of discrimination (Open Society Institute, 2005). In particular, 'practising' young Muslim women were likely to face discrimination because of their affiliation to Islam. In this regard, religion rather than race or ethnicity was recognised as being a more important marker upon which discrimination was based, echoing Allen and Nielsen's (2002) finding that individuals were being increasingly targeted on the visibility of their (perceived) Muslim identity. Further evidence of the prominence of Muslim women as targets of anti-Muslim discrimination was published in the report *Data in Focus: Muslims* by the European Union Agency for Fundamental Rights (2009). The report found that approximately 26 per cent of Muslim women across a number of different European countries had experienced discrimination in the preceding year. Weller (2011), who examined religious discrimination in Britain over the previous decade, found that Muslims experience religious discrimination with a frequency and seriousness that is proportionately greater than that experienced by those of other religions.

Evidently, 'visible' Muslims in general and veiled Muslim women in particular emerge as 'ideal' targets for those who wish to attack a symbol of Islam. In this regard, the visibility of their 'Muslimness' is key to rendering them 'ideal' victims for Islamophobic attacks in public. In a report published by the European Monitoring Centre for Racism and Xenophobia, Allen and Nielsen (2002) found that the stimulant behind the vast majority of Islamophobic incidents was the fact that victims

DOI: 10.1057/9781137356154.0005

were identified as Muslims by 'visual identifiers', namely something that could be recognisably associated with Islam. Within this paradigm, the visual identifiers of Islam are the tools for identification upon which Islamophobia can be expressed and demonstrate why certain individuals and groups are more likely to become targets for hostility than others. Examples of such visual identifiers include veiled Muslim women, bearded men as well as Islamic buildings and property. However, as Allen (2010b) observes, when the visual identifiers of Islam hold such primacy in determining who or what become the targets for violence, it is veiled Muslim women in particular – possibly the most visually identifiable religious adherents in the West – who become the primary *foci* for retaliation. This ties in with the suggestions of Githens-Mazer and Lambert (2010) who documented the heightened sense of vulnerability of veiled Muslim women by virtue of their 'visible' Muslim identity in public places in London.

As of 2014, official figures and academic research indicate that anti-Muslim hate crimes are currently at record levels compared to the beginning of the decade. From the period between September 2001 and 2010 successive Crown Prosecution Service (CPS) racist incident monitoring reports highlight that Muslims accounted for more than half of all incidents of religiously aggravated offences at 54 per cent, whilst up to 60 per cent of mosques, Islamic centres and Muslim organisations suffered at least one attack (Ahmed, 2012). In 2011, over half of British Muslims reported having experienced at least one incident of Islamophobic abuse, harassment or intimidation in public (Ahmed, 2012). From April 2012 to April 2013, the Measuring Anti-Muslim Attacks project (MAMA, 2013) found that 58 per cent of all reported incidents were against Muslim women, whilst 80 per cent of the Muslim women targeted were visually identifiable as being Muslim because of their dress. Following the murder of British army soldier Drummer Lee Rigby in Woolwich, London by two Islamist extremists in May 2013, there was a clear spike in attacks on Muslims. For example, more than 140 anti-Muslim hate crime incidents were reported to the Measuring Anti-Muslim Attacks project in the 48 hours following the Woolwich murder (*The Independent*, 2013). The preceding discussion not only supports the very real existence of Islamophobia but also highlights the targeted victimisation of 'visible' Muslims and particularly of veiled Muslim women. However, even when its existence is acknowledged, Islamophobic victimisation is frequently discussed in gender-neutral ways.

DOI: 10.1057/9781137356154.0005

The gendered dimensions of Islamophobic victimisation

Despite the link between the visibility of Islam and incidents of Islamophobic victimisation in public, the vulnerability of veiled Muslim women remains a largely ignored phenomenon. It is important to recognise that issues around the 'Muslim veil' are intersectional: the term suggests that the garment in question is religious in nature but it is also gender-specific, as only Muslim women (and not Muslim men) adopt the practice of wearing it. Nevertheless, the intersection of gender and religion in relation to the 'Muslim veil' has not been adequately considered or analysed. As Vakulenko (2007) observes, there is a noticeable tendency to overlook or underestimate the connection between gender and Islamophobic victimisation. Recognition and analysis of the key role of the veil in relation to public manifestations of Islamophobia is essential in order to understand the nature and impact of this type of targeted victimisation.

At a general level, social constructions of gender are central to the imagination and reproduction of national identities whilst at a more fundamental level women may be seen as biological reproducers of members of ethnic groups and, by extension, as reproducers of boundaries of national collectivities. According to this line of thinking, women are perceived as 'the signifiers of national differences in the construction, reproduction and transformation of national categories' (Meer et al., 2010: 85). Although men are more likely to monopolise the nation's political and military representation, it is women who come to 'embody' the nation as such (Lutz, Pheonix and Yuval-Davis, 1995). From this perspective, women are seen as vehicles for transmitting national and cultural values. Ultimately, the veil emerges as the typifying content of Islam based on the premise that the practice of veiling makes the abstract and universal concept of Islam more concrete. Reflections such as these may help to explain why the image of the veiled Muslim woman has become such a visual representative of Islam.

Clearly, the veil is the most visible symbol of Islam in the West. By virtue of the fact that it draws together different anti-Muslim themes, the veil serves as a focal point for antipathy towards Islam and Muslims. In particular, the 'gendered' dimensions of Islamophobic victimisation are premised on five different, yet interrelated, arguments. First, gender precipitates anti-Muslim hostility on the basis that the wearing of the

DOI: 10.1057/9781137356154.0005

veil marks Muslim women as particularly vulnerable to Islamophobic victimisation in public. In this regard, stereotypes about Muslim women's passivity (particularly if wearing the veil) render them 'ideal subjects' against whom to enact Islamophobic attacks. As already discussed in Chapter 1, the wearing of the veil is routinely seen as an oppressive and subordinating practice which is not 'welcome' in the West. Based on the Western perspective, veiled Muslim women are routinely perceived as submissive, passive and with very little power over their lives. Thus, popular perceptions that veiled Muslim women are deemed 'passive' increase their chance of assault, thereby marking them as an 'easy' target to attack.

Secondly, despite the actual or perceived degree of agency of the wearer, the visibility of the veil in the West provokes public manifestations of Islamophobia by virtue of its symbolism as a sign of self-segregation, either imposed or chosen. Although freedom of choice and individual agency are amongst the most cherished values in contemporary Western societies, the woman who freely chooses to veil often provokes public hostility. According to Goffman (1963) individuals whose stigma is visible experience more discrimination than individuals with conceal-able stigmas. Given that the majority of Muslim women do not wear the veil, Muslim women who do wear it are likely to be perceived as having a 'controllable' stigma for choosing to wear it (Ghumman and Ryan, 2013). Correspondingly, in cases where women choose to wear the veil, they are seen as purposefully isolating themselves and rejecting Western values. As such, individuals who have such controllable stigmas are more likely to be subjected to stigmatisation based on the premise that they are perceived as being 'responsible' for their own condition. Consequently, veiled Muslim women are likely to experience Islamophobic victimisa-tion not only because of the visibility of the veil, but also because of its perceived controllability.

Thirdly, the 'refusal' of veiled Muslim women to conform to the expectation of being 'the object of the gaze' constitutes a disruption of power relations in the public sphere. It was contended in Chapter 1 that the visibility of the veil confounds public norms, partly because of the veil's message of sexual unavailability. This symbolism brings the veiled Muslim woman very visibly into the public sphere where she simply cannot walk by unnoticed. In this context the veil symbolises the sexual non-availability of Muslim women, and consequently men (and women) may find it difficult to forgive those who 'disrupt' the 'pattern of the masculine gaze' (Franks, 2000: 920). Ultimately, veiled Muslim women may be attacked for failing to conform to Western expectations of how women should behave and dress.

Fourthly, the image of the veiled Muslim woman represents 'Islam', the religion of the perpetrators of high profile terrorist attacks such as 9/11 and 7/7. In this sense, the beliefs and practices of veiled Muslim women are unthinkingly equated with those of the terrorists: as such, attacks towards veiled Muslim women are justified because of the conflation of Islam with terrorism. Moreover, veiled Muslim women might be seen as 'terrorist' bodies on the basis that their face is covered and therefore the veil could be used as a camouflage for a terrorist. This link legitimises Islamophobic attacks toward veiled Muslim women when they are seen in public. In this context, the veil is completely separated from the individual wearing it; rather, it is seen as part of an Islamist agenda that aims to impose Sharia law in the West. The effect is to construct and maintain the particular identity and meaning ascribed to veiled Muslim bodies, thereby contributing to a hostile environment towards women whose Muslim identity is visible through the process of veiling in a non-Muslim country. Allied with the repetitive effects of erroneously linking Islam to Islamist terrorism, this rhetoric provides the justification for the targeted victimisation of veiled women whose 'Muslimness' is visible in public places.

Finally, veiled Muslim women may be targeted because they are seen as more visually 'threatening' than Muslim men as it is more difficult for their Muslim identity to be mistaken, denied, or concealed. A key theme emerging from the available research literature is that veiled Muslim women are more vulnerable to Islamophobic attacks in public because they are easily identifiable as Muslims. Indeed, respondents in Tyrer and Ahmad's (2006) study reported that men and women experience Islamophobia in different ways and this was linked to the greater visibility of Muslim women wearing the veil.[1] Afshar et al. (2005: 262) state that veiled Muslim women 'are publicly branding themselves as Muslims at a time when such a label carries the potential fear of making them vulnerable to open hostility'. In the eyes of the perpetrators, the image of the veiled Muslim woman evokes mixed emotions of fear and hostility. As such, the wearing of the veil is read in a uniform, linear manner as a practice which is adopted by the Muslim 'Other'. In this light, the image of the veiled Muslim body challenges or 'threatens' hegemonic socio-cultural norms. Along similar lines, the veil is seen as a cultural threat

DOI: 10.1057/9781137356154.0005

to 'our' way of life. It is in such a context that Islamophobic victimisation emerges as a means of responding to this 'threat'.

Collectively, these observations demonstrate that the veil has simultaneously become a 'visual identifier' of Islam and an embodiment of what is in itself stereotypically Islamophobic: namely, the veil as a symbol of Muslim 'otherness'. As such, for girls and women who adhere to Islamic dress codes which visibly mark them as Muslims, public expressions of Islamophobia are particularly salient. Against the backdrop of the 'war on terror' and the perpetual debates on the oppression of Muslim women, the visibility of the veil in the West renders the veiled Muslim woman the 'ideal' target against whom to enact Islamophobic attacks. In other words, the veil marks Muslim women more readily visible as 'soft', 'easy' and 'convenient' targets to attack. In this light, the vulnerability of veiled Muslim women *vis-à-vis* Islamophobia is premised on their perceived subordination and passivity, dangerousness and self-segregation, coupled with the visibility of their Muslim identity. This line of argument can help us to recognise that Islamophobia, implicit as it is in contemporary media, political and public discourses, offers 'us' (the 'ideal' spectators) a vehicle with which we are expected to envisage the Muslim 'Other'. In this context, manifestations of anti-Muslim hostility against 'Other' Muslim women are accepted, even expected. That said, it should be acknowledged that not every veiled Muslim woman will be a victim of Islamophobia. This observation is echoed by Mythen (2007: 466) who states:

> Being, or becoming a victim is not a neat or absolute journey. Acquiring the status of victim involves being party to a range of interactions and processes, including identification, labelling and recognition.

Essentially, becoming a victim is a social process which requires a cognitive decision by the person(s) against whom it is directed to view themselves as victims, as part of their strategy for coping with it. However, not everyone who has been victimised will necessarily regard themselves as a victim. Indeed, the research literature demonstrates that some recipients of abuse and harassment do not appreciate being referred to as 'victims' (see, for example, Bowling and Phillips, 2002). Moreover, some people may not recognise that they have been victimised. Islamophobic victimisation may form such an intrinsic part of their everyday experience that the individuals or groups against whom it is directed consider it to be 'normal' and as a result, may not appreciate that they have been

DOI: 10.1057/9781137356154.0005

victimised. At the same time, the term 'victim' is not always an appropriate one to use when referring to the lived experiences of veiled Muslim women, not least because it tends to perpetuate an imagery of inevitability about the process of 'Othering' and passivity on the part of the recipient. However, in the context of the present discussion, the term has been used deliberately to give emphasis to the 'invisibility' of Muslim women as victims of anti-Muslim hostility, thereby raising awareness about the vulnerability of women who look 'different', and overtly 'Muslim', in the current climate of Islamophobia.

Chapter 1 demonstrated that Islamophobia is not a distinctly post-9/11 phenomenon, but one which evolved out of Orientalism. It was argued that both colonial and contemporary stereotypes of Islam and Muslims have promoted the construction of the Muslim as 'Other' to the non-Muslim Self. Crucially in this context, a common image that resides in public perceptions of Muslim women (particularly if wearing the veil) is the image of the oppressed female body. This chapter has examined the nature and extent of Islamophobic victimisation. The review of the literature suggests that veiled Muslim women are particularly vulnerable to public manifestations of anti-Muslim hostility in the UK, as elsewhere in the West. Readers will note that we have deliberately drawn attention to the fact that Islamophobic victimisation is highly 'gendered'. In this regard, gender precipitates expressions of Islamophobia on the basis that the visibility of the veil, coupled with popular perceptions of gender oppression in Islam, marks veiled Muslim women as 'uniquely' vulnerable to verbal and physical attacks in public places in the West and elsewhere.

Note

1   This was a qualitative study of the experiences of Muslim women studying in Higher Education Institutions across the UK.

DOI: 10.1057/9781137356154.0005

3
Researching Islamophobia and the Veil

Abstract: *As outlined in previous chapters, relatively little is known about veiled Muslim women's lived experiences despite their vulnerability as victims of Islamophobia. Against this background, our research sought to improve knowledge of their targeted victimisation, which is all too often 'hidden' from academic enquiry. This chapter presents our methodology and describes the nature of qualitative research undertaken to explore these issues. A key component was the process of conducting semi-structured interviews with veiled Muslim women, key stakeholders and policy-makers in Leicester, which generated important insights into the nature, extent and impact of this victimisation. In framing the lines of enquiry of the research, emphasis was given to eliciting information from veiled Muslim women from different backgrounds in order to provide as informed and full a picture as possible. The chapter discusses the similarities and differences between the researcher and the researched which are framed by notions of insider and outsider status. We argue that being an outsider can benefit the research process by enabling the researcher to elicit detailed responses whilst maintaining a critical distance from the data.*

Zempi, Irene and Neil Chakraborti. *Islamophobia, Victimisation and the Veil.* Basingstoke: Palgrave Macmillan, 2014. DOI: 10.1057/978113735614.0006.

DOI: 10.1057/9781137356154.0006

Framing the present research study

The methodology used as the basis of our empirical research was comprised of the following strands: individual and focus group interviews with veiled Muslim women; individual interviews with local key stakeholders and policy-makers; and a micro-ethnographic approach which is described below. The purpose of this research was to shed light on the experiences of veiled Muslim women as victims of Islamophobia in public places in Leicester and elsewhere. It is important to recognise that veiled Muslim women are rarely included within studies of victimisation despite their increased levels of vulnerability in public – a factor which in itself exacerbates their marginalisation from both academic discourses and mainstream society. Moreover, the need for researching Islamophobia has become more urgent in a post-9/11 climate on the basis that Muslims in general and veiled Muslim women in particular are perceived as 'ideal' targets of anti-Muslim attacks in the eyes of the perpetrators. Popular perceptions of veiled Muslim women as submissive, oppressed and subjugated render them 'easy' and 'soft' targets to attack thereby increasing their vulnerability in public places. This aspect of the research study becomes even more important in the wake of legislation banning the niqab in public places in European countries such as France, Belgium and Italy.

The fieldwork was conducted in the city of Leicester between 2011 and 2012. It comprises of 60 individual interviews and 20 focus group interviews with veiled Muslim women who have been victims of Islamophobia in public places in Leicester and elsewhere; and 15 individual interviews with key stakeholders and policy-makers from organisations such as the Police, Victim Support, Witness Service, Crown Prosecution Service, Leicester City Council, Leicestershire County Council as well as local faith-based organisations. Of the 60 veiled Muslim women who took part in individual interviews[1], 83 per cent (n = 50) were born into Islam and 17 per cent (10) had converted to Islam, whilst the largest ethnic group of participants classified themselves as Asian (Indian, Pakistani, Bangladeshi, and Asian Other) 70 per cent (n = 42), followed by Black (either Black Caribbean, Black African, and Black Other) 13 per cent (n = 8), and White (British, Irish, and Other) 17 per cent (n = 10). The majority of participants had lived in Leicester for five years or more (67 per cent, n = 40).

DOI: 10.1057/9781137356154.0006

Leicester is located at the heart of the East Midlands of England. The 2011 Census puts the population of Leicester at approximately 330,000. Leicester residents hail from over 50 countries from across the globe, making the city one of the most ethnically and culturally diverse places in the UK. The latest Census figures reveal that 45.1 per cent of the city's residents are White British, 5.5 per cent are Other White groups, 28.3 per cent are Asian/Asian British Indian, 2.4 per cent are Asian/Asian British Pakistani, 6.4 per cent are Other Asian/Asian British groups, 6.2 per cent are Black African/Caribbean/Black British, 3.5 per cent are from Mixed/Multiple ethnic groups and 3 per cent are from 'Other' ethnic groups. This diversity is further reflected in the variety of religious and secular traditions and identities in the city: 32.4 per cent are Christian, 22.8 per cent are of 'no religion', 18.6 per cent are Muslim, 15.2 per cent are Hindu, 4.4 per cent are Sikh, 0.6 per cent follow 'other' religions, 0.2 are Buddhist and 0.1 are Jewish.[2] In relation to religious affiliation, Christians remain the largest group followed by those with 'no religion', whilst those who identify as Muslims are now the third largest group. In light of its diverse mix of cultures and faiths, Leicester is commonly depicted as the reflection of a modern, vibrant, multi-cultural city and as the UK's most ethnically harmonious city. As such, Leicester is seen as a successful model of multiculturalism both nationally and internationally. As one of the most diverse cities in the UK – and with such a sizeable population of Muslims and veil wearing women – Leicester was an ideal site in which to conduct the study.

Employing a qualitative research framework

While quantitative methods can provide useful statistical context, they can be regarded as ineffective in capturing the experiences of victimisation of 'hard-to-reach' groups. Due to cultural factors as well as feelings of 'resistance' and 'suspicion' towards non-Muslims, a quantitative study would not be able to capture the experiences, views and opinions of victims of Islamophobia due to a lack of engagement on the part of the target population. At the same time, quantitative methods fail to recognise the process of victimisation on the basis that they provide only narrowly focused snapshots of behaviour, actions and perceptions. As such, a quantitative approach would have been insufficiently sensitive to explore the targeted victimisation of veiled Muslim women.

DOI: 10.1057/9781137356154.0006

A qualitative approach recognises the dynamic nature of victimisation and the wider social processes that give rise to this victimisation. It also takes into account the perspective of the women being interviewed, establishes a high level of rapport and trust between the interviewer and the interviewees, and promotes a non-hierarchical relationship between the researcher and the researched.

The distinctiveness of qualitative research is premised on three key characteristics: it is inductivist, interpretivist, and constructionist. One of the main features of qualitative research is an inductive view of the relationship between theory and research, whereby theory is generated out of the research findings. The framework which was used to guide the analysis of data in the present study was grounded theory, where themes were allowed to emerge from the data, thereby enabling theories about the nature of Islamophobic victimisation to be generated, tested and refined during the analytical process. While this process of induction facilitated an enhanced theoretical understanding of the targeted victimisation of veiled Muslim women based upon observations from the qualitative material, some of the theories and explanations which emerged over the course of the research spurred the collection of further data in order to test these theories. This strategy of oscillation between testing emerging theories and collecting data facilitates an interplay between interpretation and theorising, and data collection. Such an approach is referred to as an iterative one (Maxfield and Babbie, 2009).

An epistemological position described as interpretivist highlights the preference for 'seeing through the eyes of the people being studied' and 'in their own setting' (Bryman, 2008). This was achieved through the use of an ethnographic approach whereby Irene wore the veil for a prolonged period of time in public places in Leicester. Clearly, the ethnographic fieldwork helped the interpretation of the data in terms of understanding veiled Muslim women's experiences as victims of Islamophobia and recognising how 'low-level' Islamophobic victimisation was embedded within their daily lives. Finally, an ontological position described as constructionist suggests that social properties are not 'phenomena out there' but outcomes of the interactions between the researcher and the researched. Symbolic interactionism suggests that the process of understanding social phenomena is not undertaken by individuals in isolation from each other but occurs in interaction with others (Bryman, 2008). This point is explored further in due course in

DOI: 10.1057/9781137356154.0006

the context of outlining the similarities and differences between the researcher and the researched.

Methodology in action: individual and focus group interviews

Qualitative interviewing provided the study with detailed and diverse insights into veiled Muslim women's experiences as victims of Islamophobia as well as information about the nature and effects of this victimisation. This was achieved through individual and focus group interviews with veiled Muslim women, and individual interviews with local key stakeholders and policy-makers. Individual interviews are used primarily when researching sensitive issues that require confidentiality and a more intimate setting for data collection, and this is especially appropriate for a 'hard-to-access' group such as veiled Muslim women. In comparison to focus groups, individual interviews can be easier to manage as the interviewer can focus on one person. This allows for easier rapport-building in the sense that the participant may be more willing to share personal information, and there is also more time to pursue interesting areas without other participants interrupting. Individual interviews can also be useful in terms of understanding the economic, socio-cultural and religious context of the target population (Hennink, Hutter and Bailey, 2011), which was highly relevant in the context of this study, as will be discussed in due course.

In addition to individual interviews, the methodology included 20 focus group interviews with veiled Muslim women who had experienced incidents of Islamophobic victimisation in public places in Leicester and elsewhere. Focus group interviews incorporate the strengths of qualitative research in terms of gathering 'rich' data whilst generating additional insights through group interactions. In the context of this particular piece of research, focus groups were used to capture the importance of interactions between the participants, particularly to generate conversation on their perspectives and experiences of Islamophobic victimisation. In this regard, the focus group method afforded the possibility of open discussion amongst veiled Muslim women with both similar and different experiences of Islamophobic victimisation whilst, at the same time, highlighting collectively held beliefs and attitudes. As such, focus group interviews allowed participants' perspectives to be revealed in

DOI: 10.1057/9781137356154.0006

ways that were different from individual interviews, particularly in terms of allowing the voices of victims of Islamophobia to be heard collectively at familiar locations such as mosques, Islamic centres and Islamic educational institutions.

Methodology in action: ethnography

In addition to individual and focus group interviews, the study also included an ethnographic element which involved Irene wearing the veil in public places in Leicester. By adopting the dress code of veiled Muslim women, the intention was to feel part of their 'reality'. From this perspective, seeing through the eyes of the research participants emerges as a crucial element in the production of knowledge. At the same time though, it is important to recognise that this approach produced subjective knowledge, which was temporarily and spatially located since it was mediated through the ethnographer's interpretation. Liamputtong (2009) observes that ethnography involves immersion in a setting with the aim of coming to experience events in the same way as the population of interest, although the degree to which this is feasible was limited within the context of this particular piece of research.

This aspect of the research did not amount to 'full-scale' ethnography as it was conducted over set periods of time during the daytime only, but rather was used as a complementary approach to generate insights beyond the scope of a more conventional approach. In the language of research methods, this fieldwork took the form of micro-ethnography. During the process Irene assumed a covert role and did not disclose the fact that she was a researcher to members of the public, which meant that members of the public were not aware of her status as a researcher and as a result would behave naturally in front of her. This covert role was essential to the success of the ethnographic research. It is highly likely that people's awareness of her status as a researcher would influence how they treated her, which would potentially mask the true dimensions of public expressions of Islamophobic prejudice.

In total Irene wore the veil for four weeks as part of her daily routine in public places in the city of Leicester such as streets, shopping centres and public means of transport. At times, the ethnographic part of the study was fraught with difficulties, and indeed in certain circumstances with danger. After wearing the veil for a few days

DOI: 10.1057/9781137356154.0006

Irene felt that she was under constant threat and as a result she had to be alert all the time whilst wearing the veil in public. The various situations that she encountered because of her perceived Muslim identity resulted in her being subjected to verbal abuse and potential physical attacks; situations that were probably 'normal' for both victims and perpetrators. She encountered numerous expressions of anti-Muslim hostility such as persistent staring, angry looks, being ignored, Islamophobic comments such as 'Terrorist', 'Muslim bomber' and 'Go back to Afghanistan', and as a result Irene felt vulnerable to physical attacks particularly in public spaces which were less crowded. Without question the ethnographic fieldwork demonstrated how 'low-level' Islamophobic victimisation is embedded within veiled Muslim women's daily lives.

Mapping the insider and outsider positions

It is important to acknowledge Irene's status as a white, Orthodox Christian, female researcher documenting veiled Muslim women's lived experiences of Islamophobic victimisation. This enables us to reflect on the relevance of core intersectional aspects of Irene's identity such as religion, gender and race in order to evaluate how knowledge is produced in the context of researcher subjectivities. Spalek (2005) points out that when the researcher holds different racial, religious and cultural positions from the researched, he or she must be aware that due to their wish to establish rapport with the participants, they might be overlooking crucial aspects of participants' lived experiences; aspects which are linked to racial, religious and cultural power hierarchies of which the researcher may be a part. Along similar lines, Garland, Spalek and Chakraborti (2006) argue that although some aspects of the researcher's self-identity may enable him or her to document the previously 'hidden' experiences of minority communities, other aspects of the researcher's self-identity can lead to the misrepresentation of those experiences, thereby serving to maintain and reproduce dominant power relations. This line of argument highlights the importance of the researcher's 'insider' or 'outsider' status and the extent to which an 'outsider' position can lead to the misrepresentation of participants' lived experiences.

In light of this, it is important to draw the parameters of the 'insider' and 'outsider' debate. The notion of 'insider' suggests that researchers

DOI: 10.1057/9781137356154.0006

who are members of minority groups have privileged access to knowledge about the experiences of these groups because of the researcher's minority status. Researchers are perceived as 'outsiders' when interviewing individuals from different ethnic, religious or cultural groups. In essence, research which is undertaken by outsiders tends to be critiqued for failing to comprehend or accurately represent the experiences of members of minority groups (Philips and Bowling, 2003). Accordingly, insiders have greater awareness and understanding of minority issues in comparison to outsiders and thus they can provide accounts of minority experiences which are genuine and legitimate. From this perspective, an insider researcher is better positioned because of his or her knowledge of the relevant patterns of social interaction required for gaining access, increasing participants' willingness to disclose personal and sensitive information, and making meaning. This line of argument suggests that the researcher must be part of the minority group he or she is researching in order to truly understand participants' experiences, particularly when researching disadvantaged or disempowered communities such as religious and ethnic minorities.

'Outsider' status

Being an insider can hold many advantages, particularly in terms of gaining access for qualitative interviewing. This aspect of the research process is important because how access is gained and granted influences the data collection, including establishing rapport between the researcher and the researched. The gatekeepers and the participants themselves can deny access to researchers who are perceived as outsiders. For example, participants might have assumptions regarding certain characteristics of the outsider researcher which ultimately obstruct access. In addition, they might be wondering 'why us' whilst resisting any scrutiny 'by anyone not on their side' (Shah, 2004). Clearly, 'getting in' or gaining access for qualitative interviewing can be challenging depending upon the perceptions of participants and gatekeepers regarding outsider researchers.

   In the context of this particular piece of research, being a non-Muslim researcher meant that access to potential participants was not always guaranteed. However, engaging with local Muslim organisations as well as community leaders eased access to veiled Muslim women. As Keval (2009) points out, gatekeepers wield considerable power in validating

DOI: 10.1057/9781137356154.0006

or rejecting identities. In this sense, having a partially validated identity made the rest of the fieldwork less problematic and gave 'the green light' to veiled Muslim women in the local community to participate in the study. Moreover, key informants such as veiled Muslim women from the local community played an important role in designing the field-work in terms of using religiously and culturally appropriate language and behaviour. For example, attention to dress and demeanour was an important consideration throughout the fieldwork, particularly when visiting mosques, Muslim schools and Islamic community centres. In the context of researching minority communities, Phillips and Bowling (2003) argue that the involvement of members of those communities in all stages of the process increases the chances of making the correct fieldwork choices. This approach enables the researcher to break down any cultural, religious or racial barriers that may exist between the researcher and the researched (Garland et al., 2006).

However, although relevant contacts might be helpful in terms of gaining access and making appropriate fieldwork choices, the quality of interview data will still depend upon 'getting on' with the partici-pants – a task which demands relevant knowledge and skills. Following this line of argument, agreeing to be interviewed is an initial phase that can be achieved through personal efforts, contacts or negotiations but 'getting on' with the participants could be problematic in the absence of insider's knowledge. In the words of Shah (2004: 569), 'Learning to be a good researcher, to avoid assumptions based on familiarity, and to bring a critical eye to the research context is a developmental process, but cultural knowledge is a matter of *habitus*, which cannot be acquired except by living.' Echoing the same viewpoint Garland et al. (2006) argue that examining the needs and experiences of religious minority commu-nities can be problematic, especially when the researcher holds only a basic knowledge of the particular faith that participants identify with.

By implication therefore, attempting to understand the impact of religiously motivated hate crime upon victims can be problematic, particularly when the researcher is an outsider. This raises the question of whether it is necessary for researchers to belong to the same religious group as their population of interest. Within the present study, we would argue that Irene's outsider status as a non-Muslim researcher proved to benefit the research rather than an obstacle. By being conscious of her outsider status, she used it as a tool through which to gain detailed accounts from participants, and to ensure rigorous analysis by

DOI: 10.1057/9781137356154.0006

maintaining a critical distance from the data. In other words, Irene used her outsider status as a non-Muslim researcher, and to this extent her relative lack of religious and cultural knowledge of Islam, in order to gain 'rich' interview data. Instead of relying upon her knowledge of issues regarding Islam and the Muslim veil developed outside of the interview context, Irene adopted a strategy of deliberately presenting herself as a researcher who was largely unfamiliar with these issues. Rather than downplaying her outsider status, she emphasised the differences between herself and the participants by confirming her non-Muslim background and used this as a means through which to elicit detailed and in-depth answers from them.

Fielding (2008) argues that it can be useful to come across as some-what naive and relatively ignorant so that participants describe their experiences to the researcher in detail. In light of Irene's apparent limited knowledge of Islam, participants were keen to describe central elements of their religion in relation to the veil, which placed them in the role of the 'experts' or 'educators'. It is highly likely that this strategy of portray-ing religious and cultural ignorance on her part empowered participants by putting them in a position of authority. Tinker and Armstrong (2008) argue that putting less confident participants in a position of authority encourages them to talk more freely, thereby eliciting more comprehen-sive interview data.

Research on interviewer effects indicates that some participants might speak more freely to an interviewer of a different ethnic or religious group (Tinker and Armstrong, 2008). Under this idea, participants may choose to withhold their views and experiences from a person who shares their value systems and therefore poses the risk of judging them negatively. Moreover, some individuals may choose not to disclose sensi-tive information to an interviewer of the same faith because they fear that he or she might reveal elements of the interview to other members of their community. This highlights the extent to which some partici-pants may be reluctant to share sensitive information with a person who poses the possibility of being judgemental due to a shared knowledge of religion or culture.

Furthermore, the researchers' closeness to the subject of investigation can blunt their criticality, causing them to take for granted aspects which are familiar to them, and this can have implications for the interview process. Drawing on their status, insider researchers are in a position of 'knowing' certain issues which means that such issues are not worth

DOI: 10.1057/9781137356154.0006

spelling out because they are to be taken for granted (Keval, 2009). This suggests that insider researchers might not ask questions that they feel are too insignificant or too obvious. For example, had a Muslim researcher asked 'Why do you wear the veil?' participants might have felt confused that the researcher, someone who shared their religion and knowledge of it, needed something so basic spelled out. It is likely that questions posed by an insider researcher could have been met with limited responses on the basis that participants might have felt that there is no need to explain their views and experiences of Islamophobic victimisation in detail.

With respect to the data analysis, the outsider researcher may bring analytical objectivity to the study. Tinker and Armstrong (2008) argue that outsider researchers are not 'contaminated' by bias and prejudice, and as a result they are more objective than insider researchers. Perceiving oneself as holding similar values or beliefs to participants may lead the insider researcher to assume a particular interpretation of the data, whilst a sense of distance enables the outsider researcher to remain detached and view the data critically. Following this line of thought, an insider status might prevent researchers from approaching their data analysis with the necessary criticality because of their closeness to the subject of investigation. In contrast, outsider researchers may bring a 'fresh' perspective, one which highlights key aspects of a particular religion or culture.

'Insider' status

Throughout interviews and focus group discussions, Irene was aware of her position as a white researcher and of the possibility that some participants might have seen her as the 'oppressor' on the basis of her ethnic and non-Muslim identity. Adler and Adler (2001) highlight that if participants perceive themselves as marginalised and vulnerably positioned by the white society, they might be reluctant to share information with a researcher who is 'one of them'. In this context, agreeing to be researched by a white researcher becomes a political decision which impacts upon the data made available to the outsider researcher. This decision may not necessarily be based upon the colour divide but upon what 'white' represents for black and South Asian communities that have been historically discriminated and racially abused based on their perceived 'difference' (Shah, 2004).

DOI: 10.1057/9781137356154.0006

Similarly, Phillips and Bowling (2003) argue that 'white' is the norm or standard against which ethnic minorities are to be judged, while Spalek (2005) refers to the invisibility of 'whiteness' in this context, whereby being white is considered to be 'normal', 'neutral' and 'common-sense' rather than a racial identity and a particular lens through which the world is viewed and experienced. To complicate matters further many white, non-Muslim Western social commentators and journalists have promoted false images of Islam and as a result some participants might have viewed Irene as being a part of this 'white, Western, establishment' (Spalek, 2005: 411). With this in mind, she decided to draw from an aspect of her identity that could constitute 'the oppressed' – that is her gender.

In this sense, Irene used her gender identity to establish rapport and trust with the veiled Muslim women who took part in the study. This has parallels with the approach taken by Spalek (2002) who when documenting Black Muslim women's experiences of victimisation and the management of their personal safety drew upon her position as a woman in order to establish rapport, since her racial and religious identity differed from those of the research participants. This approach is based on the notion that there is a special woman-to-woman connection between female researchers and female participants which encourages the latter to disclose sensitive information. The difficulties of using a male researcher for this kind of research should also be acknowledged. The principle of avoiding contact with 'non-mahram' men is pivotal for Muslim women who wear the veil. According to the Quran and the Sunnah (the way of life of Prophet Muhammad), free-mixing and socialisation between unrelated, non-mahram men and women is strictly forbidden in Islam, at least as a general rule, unless a woman has a mahram in her presence such as her husband, father, brother or son. However, the presence of other male family members during the interview could potentially limit the extent to which participants could disclose their experiences of Islamophobic victimisation to a male interviewer. This shows that being a female researcher was crucial in the present study.

Assessing the insider versus outsider debate

The preceding discussion has shown that the status of the researcher as an insider or outsider has great significance for all phases of the

DOI: 10.1057/9781137356154.0006

research process including access, data collection and making meaning, particularly in a qualitative research context. An improved understanding of both positions enables us to recognise benefits, limitations and to develop informed practices accordingly. At the same time though, there is more to the research process than either insider or outsider status. A simple binary rendition of the relationship between the researcher and the researched is not sufficient to explore its complexities (Keval, 2009). Rather, the relationship can be characterised by fluidity and constant negotiations of actual and perceived identities. A static and restrictive construction of the 'knower' status compared to 'stranger' status is not useful both empirically and analytically. Rather than locating these positions as exclusively positive or negative, it is important to examine these positions as possibilities for involvement in the setting and a chance to critically engage with different forms of identity.

Young (2004) observes that such a binary system requires decisions to be made about precisely where the boundaries of certain groups lie and whether those on the margins of groups fall inside or outside. Consistent with this view, Tinker and Armstrong (2008) highlight that a key problem with notions of insiders and outsiders is that such a system mandates the classification of people into categories whilst at the same time forcing researchers to identify themselves as either insiders or outsiders of a series of groups. This means that the insider/outsider classification promotes essentialist categorisations of certain groups whilst neglecting the significant differences within, as well as between, groups. Collectively, this framework fails to take into account the complexities of the multiple identities of researchers and of participants which may preclude absolute religious, cultural and racial matching. Researchers can differ from, or be similar to, research participants in various ways including religion (and the degree of practising religion), race and ethnicity, gender, age, socio-economic status or sexuality, to name but some. A similarity in one of these areas does not necessarily render the researcher an insider, just as a difference in one area does not necessarily make the researcher an outsider (Tinker and Armstrong, 2008). Garland et al. (2006) suggest that if we wish to create knowledge that moves beyond essentialist discourses we must move beyond an essentialist view of the researcher, and recognise the complexity of subject positions that a researcher occupies and how these might influence the research process. Ultimately, it is imperative that we break out of the boundaries

DOI: 10.1057/9781137356154.0006

of religious, racial and cultural parochialism, and acknowledge and respond to diversity in research.

In conclusion, this chapter has documented the methodology that we used to explore veiled Muslim women's experiences as victims of hate and prejudice. It outlined the rationale for using individual and focus group interviews as the two primary sources of data collection: as noted above, individual, in-depth interviews allow for 'rich' data to be collected whilst focus group interviews can generate additional insights through group interactions. Equally, the chapter has shown how the micro-ethnographic phase allowed the research to take a brief but important glimpse into the lived realities of veiled Muslim women. The chapter has also looked at the role of the researcher as an 'insider' or 'outsider'. In the context of the present study it was argued that being an outsider can benefit the research process by enabling the researcher to ask the kinds of interview questions which would otherwise be 'off-limits', to minimise participants' fear of being judged and to maintain a critical distance from the interview data.

Notes

1   It is not possible to provide any demographic information about the veiled Muslim women who took part in the focus group interviews because Irene was not allowed to note their personal details by the relevant gatekeepers.

2   5.6 per cent did not state their religion.

DOI: 10.1057/9781137356154.0006

4
Uncovering Islamophobic Victimisation

Abstract: *In a post-9/11 climate, veiled Muslim women face an increased risk of abuse and hostility by virtue of the visibility of their Muslim identity. This chapter examines the nature of Islamophobic victimisation and illustrates the different forms of abuse that veiled Muslim women experience in public. It reveals the regularity with which actual and potential victims become repeat targets of verbal and physical attacks. The chapter also uncovers 'invisible' forms of Islamophobic victimisation including persistent staring and stalking which are rarely recognised or acknowledged as such by victims. Crucially, recognising Islamophobic victimisation as a process signifies that it is 'part and parcel' of veiled Muslim women's everyday life, and this reinforces the sense of constant risk for actual and potential victims. Although it is difficult to quantify this victimisation, the chapter identifies how commonplace these experiences are and highlights the relevance of factors such as space in terms of rendering Muslim women more or less vulnerable.*

Zempi, Irene and Neil Chakraborti. *Islamophobia, Victimisation and the Veil.* Basingstoke: Palgrave Macmillan, 2014. DOI: 10.1057/9781137356154.0007.

Nature of Islamophobic victimisation

Verbal abuse

Throughout interviews and focus group discussions participants were familiar with the term 'Islamophobia' and had a relatively good understanding of what the term meant – that is, hostility towards Islam and Muslims. A couple of participants had not heard of the term before but it became apparent that they had nonetheless experienced incidents that could be described as Islamophobic victimisation. Regardless of their level of understanding of the term, participants related many incidents that they had personally experienced to this victimisation. They reported that some of this hostility was manifested in terms of physical violence although most took the form of verbal abuse. In particular, verbal abuse from strangers in public places – streets, shopping centres, on trains and on buses – was a clear feature of their everyday life.[1] This is consistent with the views of Githens-Mazer and Lambert (2010) who found that manifestations of Islamophobia are invariably random in nature on the basis that (perceived) Muslims are randomly targeted when they are seen in public.

Within the present study, respondents described walking on the street and being unexpectedly verbally or physically attacked. Every single one of the participants stated that they had suffered verbal abuse including name-calling, swearing, threats of physical violence and verbal abuse disguised as jokes. Underlying all these forms of verbal abuse was a clear sense of anti-Muslim sentiment and this was made apparent through the language used by the perpetrators. There was a strong feeling amongst participants that an anti-Muslim component was indeed part of this abuse. Correspondingly, the use of anti-Muslim language was the most common reason given by participants for believing that these incidents were motivated by Islamophobia. For example, when explaining the basis for their perception that the incident was Islamophobic, participants pointed out that the perpetrators had actually referred to Islam or the veil. The second most common reason for believing that these incidents were motivated by Islamophobia was participants' belief that these attacks would not have happened to them if they were not dressed in veil.

Participants made explicit reference to the type of language used by the perpetrators, which signified their motivations for the attack. For example, they had been called names such as 'terrorists', 'Muslim bombers'

DOI: 10.1057/9781137356154.0007

and 'suicide bombers', which indicate the perpetrators' perceptions of veiled Muslim women as a security or terrorist threat. Seen in this light, the veiled female body offers a visual representation of 'radical' Islam, at least in the eyes of the perpetrators. Along similar lines, the following comments demonstrate that the wearing of the veil was perceived as a camouflage for a terrorist.

Have you got a bomb under there?

Nisha, 28 years old

Are you carrying belts full of explosives?

Jahidah, 22 years old

When are you going to blow us up?

Shelina, 36 years old

Why are you dressed like that? Are you a suicide bomber?

Amtullah, 24 years old

Importantly, participants argued that even if they were not seen to be involved in a terrorist plot – because veiled Muslim women are supposedly too oppressed, uneducated and incapable of autonomy – they were nevertheless perceived as the mothers of future home-grown terrorists; hence perpetrators often called them names such as 'Bin Laden's wife'. Research highlights that 'visible' Muslims and veiled Muslim women in particular are often targeted because their abusers hold the view that all Muslims are terrorists or terrorist sympathisers (see also Choudhury, 2010; Githens-Mazer and Lambert, 2010). Additionally, participants described examples of verbal abuse which illustrated the racist and xenophobic sentiments of the perpetrators, as the following comments indicate:

Go back to your country, you don't belong here!

Nadia, 29 years old

Go back to where from you came from! Go back to Afghanistan!

Focus group participant

If you want Sharia go back to Iraq!

Nabeeha, 22 years old

Take it off! You are in my country now!

Layla, 38 years old

In the eyes of their abusers, veiled Muslim women are seen as immigrants who 'don't belong' despite the fact that they have been born or largely raised in the UK. Within this paradigm, the wearing of the veil marks an unwelcome religious, cultural and racial presence (Grillo and Shah, 2013). Crucially, this type of language can be linked to the alleged 'Islamification' of the UK. In the current climate of economic instability – and again, in the eyes of their detractors – Muslims are supposedly 'taking over' Britain and as a result the visibility of the veil poses a 'threat' to national identity. This discourse mirrors certain European government policies that are designed to 'domesticate' Islam. For example, the banning of the hijab in schools in France in 2004, the banning of Minarets in Switzerland in 2009 and more recently the banning of the veil in public in European countries such as France, Belgium and Italy, are clear examples of assimilation policies which aim to eradicate the visibility of Islam in the West. Even in countries such as the UK where there is no formal (national) ban on either hijabs or niqabs, the wearing of the veil is routinely seen as an unwillingness (whether intentionally or unintentionally) to integrate into British society. Certainly, in this thinking integration means assimilation.

Moreover, there were incidents where the nature of the verbal abuse suggested both racist and Islamophobic hatred. At one level, this indicates that the targeted victimisation of veiled Muslim women can be attributed to Islamophobic attitudes as well as to racist and xenophobic sentiments by virtue of the fact that these elements are often inextricably intertwined. In this context Islamophobia, racism and xenophobia become mutually reinforcing phenomena, and hostility against veiled Muslim women should also be considered in the context of a more general climate of hostility towards 'otherness'. However, this is not to overlook the fact that veiled Muslim women have been victims of targeted violence because their abusers have been motivated either solely or partially by other factors. For example, the sight of the veiled female body might provoke anger in some men who are used to 'seeing' in the public space.

> We are very different to the average non-Muslim woman. We are doing everything that the media tells us we shouldn't be doing in terms of how women should dress.
>
> Roukia, 27 years old

> In Western societies men are used to seeing women in all their glory really, aren't they? I think men appreciate the fact that they can see a woman's face and that they can see her figure. They probably feel deprived of this

DOI: 10.1057/9781137356154.0007

opportunity because they can't assess a Muslim woman in the same way that they can assess a Christian, Sikh or Hindu woman.

Aleena, 28 years old

In this sense, the face and body of a woman is an object of sexual attraction and when these are covered it disrupts public expectations of how women should behave and dress in public in order to visually 'please' men. This emphasises the 'appropriate' feminine sexuality, which ensures that the behaviour and attire of women are strictly monitored (Dwyer, 1999). This was evident in incidents where participants were subjected to remarks of a sexual nature which were often accompanied by menacing staring, sexual gestures, whistling and kissing noises made by (mostly white young) men on the street.

Give us a flash!

Alima, 20 years old

Show me what you're wearing under there!

Ruqiia, 17 years old

This form of sexual harassment is motivated by a male gaze that desires possession of women's bodies and 'wants to see' (Al-Saji, 2010). As a solution to this 'problem', perpetrators demanded that participants uncovered their face and body by shouting 'Take it off' and 'Show me your face'. In particular, one participant was approached by a man who shouted:

I want to cut that black thing off your face!

Halimah, 19 years old

These findings lend weight to the view that there is a male desire to uncover the female Muslim body which is covered in public (Dwyer, 1999). This was also evident in the following comments made exclusively by male perpetrators:

Why don't you take it off? Are you not hot in that?

Jahidah, 22 years old

What's that on your face? Why are you covering it?

Sarah, 31 years old

Why do you have a mask on? Are you really ugly under there?

Focus group participant

As is clear from the last quote given above, participants were subjected to sexist remarks and this mirrors a society that glorifies physical beauty. Furthermore, participants reported that they were used as a form of

DOI: 10.1057/9781137356154.0007

entertainment. For example, perpetrators called them names such as 'ninja', 'Catwoman', 'Batman', 'Darth Vader', 'ghost woman', 'letterbox' and 'postbox'. In a similar fashion, perpetrators asked them sarcastic questions such as:

> Is it Halloween?
> Where's your samurai?

Focus group participants

As is clear from these comments, verbal abuse targeted at veiled Muslim women can also be disguised as a joke. Additionally, participants revealed that they had been subjected to swearing such as 'Muslim bitch', 'Muslim whore' and 'Fuck off'. Participants stated that sometimes people on the street – mainly older white English women – made comments such as 'disgusting', 'silly', 'move further' and 'get away from here' in order to express their disapproval of the wearing of the veil 'in their country'. In some cases, people on the street purposefully made negative comments about the veil so that participants could hear them. Such incidents included people saying to each other:

> I agree with the veil ban in France.

Alia, 34 years old

> I'm glad that I don't have to wear that!

Zareena, 22 years old

> What's behind there?

Mona, 38 years old

Though alarming enough when taken in isolation, these examples of verbal abuse were made all the more harrowing by the fact that they were sometimes accompanied by physical abuse.

Physical abuse

As discussed in Chapter 2, gendered and essentialised perceptions of veiled Muslim women as oppressed and powerless coupled with popular stereotypes of Muslims as terrorists or terrorist sympathisers render veiled Muslim women 'acceptable' targets for violent attacks in public. Correspondingly, participants described being aware that the wearing of the veil made them identifiable as Muslims and as a result the physical abuse that they suffered in public was a direct implication of the practice of veiling. In this regard, incidents of physical abuse included attempted and actual physical assaults (including taking the veil off), pushing,

DOI: 10.1057/9781137356154.0007

shoving, being spat at and even incidents where passing vehicles had attempted to run them over.

> Taking the veil off and getting slapped in the face; that was in Lincolnshire.
>
> Iman, 37 years old

> I was six months pregnant with my first baby and a white man elbowed me in the stomach when I was in the queue at Boots in Coventry.
>
> Kalila, 29 years old

> I was beaten up in the park [in Southampton]. Nobody stepped in to help me.
>
> Salimah, 22 years old

> I was walking on London Road [in Leicester] and this man was driving a van. Instead of going straight he saw me wearing the niqab and he came straight to me, knocked the pavement, nearly crashed into me and then drove off.
>
> Focus group participant

Participants also described incidents where people on the street or from moving cars had thrown at them eggs, stones, alcohol, water bombs, bottles, take-away food and rubbish. The following quotations are just some of the many examples from participants' accounts that help to illustrate this point.

> I've had cups of tea thrown at me from a van. There was a building firm on my street and I was going to the mosque [in Leicester] and the man looked out of his window, had his cup of tea and threw it on me. When I complained he started swearing at me. He said 'Don't make it a big deal, fuck off'.
>
> Yasmine, 28 years old

> I was waiting at the bus stop [in Peterborough] and some lads threw a lit cigarette on my jilbab.
>
> Nadia, 29 years old

Generally speaking, physical abuse is the most easily recognised form of abuse by victims. However, despite the seriousness of the aforementioned attacks, they were not always interpreted as forms of physical abuse *per se* by participants, especially if they had not sustained serious physical injuries. Instead, participants understood this violence as 'part and parcel' of wearing the veil in a post-9/11 era; hence they did not report these incidents to the police. Similar to racism and hate crime, manifestations of Islamophobia form a part of victims' everyday activities and this reality makes it difficult for victims to recognise or acknowledge the different forms of Islamophobic abuse as such (Bowling, 2003). Given that participants were multiple and repeat victims of Islamophobia, incidents of intimidation and abuse were found to be 'normal' for the majority of

DOI: 10.1057/9781137356154.0007

them. In line with the suggestions of authors such as Kelly (1987) and Bowling (1999; 2003) participants found it difficult to talk specifically about separate incidents of Islamophobic victimisation as this was seen as a problem that they faced on a daily basis in public. This necessitates looking at the complexity of veiled Muslim women's experiences rather than looking at them individually.

'Invisible' forms of Islamophobic victimisation

In addition to incidents of verbal and physical abuse, participants also described 'invisible' forms of Islamophobic victimisation, which might be best described as subtle and potentially more pervasive manifestations of Islamophobia. This can be the case where Islamophobia is manifested in a less overt manner than that typically associated with Islamophobic incidents and this highlights the importance of appreciating Islamophobic victimisation as a continuum rather than as one-off incidents. Correspondingly, none of the behaviour listed below would be defined in law (or by the participants themselves) as Islamophobic victimisation. For example, unnecessary or persistent staring was a common theme which underpinned participants' accounts as they described their experiences in public.

> If staring could kill, I would be dead by now.
>
> Focus group participant

> Other students look at me and think 'She is probably going to blow us up one day'.
>
> Aliyah, 18 years old

> When you enter Highcross [shopping centre in Leicester] people will normally hold the door for you, but they will not hold the door for me.
>
> Sabah, 27 years old

> It can be done in subtle ways. People might say 'Do you need a translator?' and talk to me really slowly or very loudly.
>
> Nimah, 28 years old

As the last quotation shows, common perceptions that veiled Muslim women do not speak English (since they are all immigrants) are further illustrations of 'invisible' Islamophobic victimisation. Other examples included being monitored at shops. In particular, several participants found themselves being followed around in shops by security officers who feared that participants might have stolen something because they were veiled.

DOI: 10.1057/9781137356154.0007

> Once I was in Morrisons in Manchester and the security officer kept walking around me and I said to him 'Is something wrong? You keep walking around me'. He said 'No, I am just monitoring' and I said 'But why do you keep walking around me?' and he said 'Because of you being covered like this, it is very easy for you to take things'. I said 'To take things? In other words you're saying that it is easy for me to steal?'
>
> Rahimah, 44 years old

Moreover, a couple of participants reported that people sometimes took photographs of them (without asking their permission) whilst others revealed that they had been victims of stalking, illustrations of which are presented below.

> I was walking on the street [in London] and this guy was following me. He was saying 'Come on, show me your face, show me your face' and after a few streets I took my niqab off and showed him my face. I was so scared that I took it off. After a couple of streets down I put it back on again.
>
> Salimah, 22 years old

> I was walking in town [in Leicester] and this man followed me home. He saw I was a single woman in the house with a child. I didn't have money to buy the curtains. He used to come and knock on the door. I told the Council what was going on and they gave me a house in another estate.
>
> Johara, 35 years old

Furthermore, participants reported that they were often treated as 'second class' citizens in the sense that people acted as if they were 'invisible'. This sense of 'invisibility' is in line with the targeted victimisation of certain groups or individuals who are judged to be 'different' and whose perceived disadvantages make them appear an 'easy target' (Chakraborti and Garland, 2012). Hate crime perpetrators routinely perceive their targets as weak, defenceless, powerless or with a limited capacity to resist. Certainly, while being 'different' does not automatically mean that someone is singled out for harassment or abuse, it can mean that those in vulnerable situations are at heightened risk of victimisation (Chakraborti and Garland, 2012). Accordingly, participants reported that some bus drivers refused to stop or open the doors for them when standing at bus stops on their own. Other participants reported that they had been ignored or refused to be served in shops, as exemplified by the following dialogue in the context of a focus group interview.

> Participant A: Sometimes when I go to the shops and I'm waiting to pay, the people who are serving me pretend they can't see me because my face is

DOI: 10.1057/9781137356154.0007

covered and they'll serve other customers. If I was a white woman wearing Western clothes they wouldn't really ignore me.

Participant B: I've been ignored in shops too. I was going to the till and I wasn't called although they were free and I said 'Excuse me, I'm standing here'.

Focus group participants

Pattern of Islamophobic victimisation

The findings described above show that experiences of Islamophobic victimisation can take a variety of different forms which may not be recognised or acknowledged as serious or even Islamophobic *per se* unless seen in context as part of the broader processes of targeted abuse and hostility that feature within veiled Muslim women's everyday lives. From this perspective, the targeted victimisation of veiled Muslim women is an everyday phenomenon which can be better understood as a process rather than as 'one-off' or incidental occurrences. This ties in with the suggestions of Williams and Tregidga (2013) who found that targeted victimisation was serial rather than singular. As such, understanding Islamophobic victimisation as a process highlights the ongoing nature of this form of targeted violence in a way that events-oriented constructions of Islamophobic victimisation fail to account for, and this would certainly seem to be an appropriate way in which to view the experiences of Islamophobia described by participants in this study.

For the majority of participants conceiving of Islamophobic victimisation as 'normal' was based on the fact that it happened 'almost daily', although there were certain factors which determined the frequency of the abuse. For example, if participants were accompanied by a male companion, they were less likely to be verbally or physically attacked. This is in line with the suggestions of the Open Society Foundations (2011) who found that veiled Muslim women in France were less likely to suffer abuse when they were walking on the street with a male relative. Within the present study, participants pointed out that although abuse and hostility was almost an everyday occurrence it was also random in the sense that it could happen anytime and anywhere, as exemplified by the following comments:

It's very common but it's quite random as well. Like today I didn't expect an old man to give me abuse on my way here [to the Department of Criminology, University of Leicester where the interview took place].

Alima, 20 years old

DOI: 10.1057/9781137356154.0007

I don't think there is a week that goes by without anything. If I went out every day to town, I'd definitely be getting something happening to me daily. Either ignoring, name-calling, pushing, shoulder turning or nose being held up. I don't know why. I don't smell. I have a bath. I don't know why people treat me like that. I don't think there's ever been a year, a month, a week or even a day when nothing, absolutely nothing has happened.

Layla, 38 years old

From an intersectional perspective, a picture emerges whereby perceived 'weaknesses' such as physical disabilities, language difficulties, ethnicity, age, physical shape and size increase the risk of being attacked. In this context, intersectionality can be understood as a nexus of identities that work together to render veiled Muslim women an 'easy' target to attack, especially in the minds of their abusers. This means that some veiled Muslim women may seem more vulnerable due to certain aspects of their identity coupled with the visibility of their Muslim identity. This is a point worth noting as it helps us to recognise that veiled Muslim women who have experienced Islamophobia will all have their own distinct individual experiences in addition to common patterns of this victimisation. During the course of individual and focus group interviews it became apparent that participants who were very young or very old, and those who had 'visible' physical or mental disabilities (including speech or language difficulties) felt very vulnerable, partly because they would not be able to defend themselves. In a similar vein, other participants felt that their body size also contributed to their vulnerability and victimisation, as the following comment indicates:

I consider myself short and attacking a small woman like me is a very cowardly act.

Shelina, 36 years old

Comments like this suggest that hate crime research needs to be more attuned to the intersectional nature of identity (see also Chakraborti and Garland, 2012). Indeed, and as the present study has shown, veiled Muslim women may be targeted not just for their group membership but because they are stereotypically perceived as 'easy' and 'soft' targets. This lends weight to Chakraborti and Garland's (2012) argument that perceived vulnerability and 'difference', rather than identity and group membership alone, are relevant factors in the commission of hate

DOI: 10.1057/9781137356154.0007

offences. They note that the intersections between a range of identity characteristics – including sexual orientation, ethnicity, disability, age, class, mental health, bodily shape and appearance – are seldom given adequate recognition within the domains of hate crime scholarship and policy. Similarly, Moran and Sharpe (2004) and Perry (2001) suggest that gay and transgendered people may be targeted because they too 'stand out' from accepted gender norms, while Hodkinson (2002) argues that male goths are harassed due to their 'effeminate' appearance as well as their membership of an alternative subculture, leaving them especially vulnerable through this intersection of two aspects of their identity. As such, it is not simply the visibility of their Muslim identity that renders veiled Muslim women vulnerable; rather, they may be targeted because of how their Muslim identity intersects with other aspects of their self, and with other situational factors and context, to make them vulnerable in the eyes of their abusers.

The significance of geography

Outside of London, the East Midlands – and Leicester in particular – is one of the most diverse regions of contemporary Britain whether considered demographically, geographically, ethnically or religiously. Leicester is seen as inclusive, multicultural and is heralded both nationally and internationally as a city of harmony and good practice. A large number of participants had decided to move to Leicester from other parts of the UK (and even from other European countries such as France) in the belief that Leicester would provide a better life for them and their families.

Indeed, Leicester provides Muslims with an authentic Islamic lifestyle based on its extensive infrastructure: veils, mosques with minarets, madrasas (Islamic educational institutions), halal shops and Muslim cemeteries. In the words of Sallah (2010: 18), one can 'feel and breathe Islam' in Leicester by virtue of its vibrant and thriving Muslim community. In light of this, participants felt confident that they would be safe to practise the veil in Leicester because of its high population of Muslims. This ties in with the suggestions of Githens-Mazer and Lambert (2010) who found that Muslims are at less risk of attack when they are in areas of high Muslim population. For most participants, hostility was a regular feature of living in communities unfamiliar with 'difference' but they

DOI: 10.1057/9781137356154.0007

soon realised that Islamophobia exists even within a multicultural city such as Leicester, albeit to a lesser degree than other cities in the UK (or elsewhere in Europe). As the following comments illustrate, there were mixed feelings about notions of safety in Leicester.

> It is worse elsewhere but there are racist people even in Leicester. We moved to Leicester because it's a safer community here. It's better for our children as well. I didn't want my daughters seeing all the hostility I saw in Coventry. Leicester is more tolerant but there is still Islamophobia.
>
> Madihah, 36 years old

> In Glasgow when I go shopping people turn and look at me. I feel they want to let me know that I'm different from everybody else because of my veil. But the English are worse than the Scottish. The Scottish, they may be racist but they are more jovial, it's not with hatred, it's not with a sense of repulsion or a sense of vindictiveness. They'll be racist towards you as a joke and you can joke back with them. In Glasgow I'll get a lot more stares but I won't get as much abuse. In the whole time I've been in Leicester, I've had more abuse than I had in Glasgow.
>
> Rasheeda, 38 years old

> My husband chose Leicester. We had to leave [the Netherlands] because my kids were growing up in an environment where people were shouting at me, pushing me. I'm sure it will happen here but not as often as it would happen there. We are a bit more sheltered here but no matter how diverse a place is, it's always going to happen.

> I don't understand why everyone says Leicester is safe. It's much easier to do niqab in Birmingham.
>
> Focus group participants

It is important to note that the level of abuse that participants faced depended upon whether they were in their local community or whether they were leaving their 'comfort zone', for instance by taking the bus to go to less familiar areas that did not accommodate 'difference'. For example, some participants referred to 'no-go zones' for Muslims in Leicester such as the traditionally white areas of Braunstone, Beaumont Leas, Saffron Lane, New Park, Hamilton and even Leicester City Centre where they would mix with 'outsiders' – that is, non-Muslim residents and visitors to Leicester.

Furthermore, participants stated that the UK was more tolerant than other European countries such as France, Italy, Germany and Greece but also Muslim countries such as Egypt and Turkey. This ties in with the suggestions of Scott-Baumann (2011) who argued that the UK provides a

DOI: 10.1057/9781137356154.0007

more veil-friendly environment than many European countries such as France where the hijab is banned in schools and within the civil service, and the niqab is banned in public. Similarly, Sallah (2010) found that Muslims felt more 'accepted' in Leicester in comparison to their experiences of living elsewhere before settling in Leicester. At the same time though, traditional Islamic States such as Saudi Arabia, Kuwait, Qatar, Bahrain, Oman and Yemen were seen by many participants as the 'ideal' country for practising Muslims to live in.

> When I went to Athens on holiday I did notice that I got a lot more stares there than I did in the UK. Nobody said anything but it was obvious that people were making a point of looking at me. I tried to smile[2] to people but they just blanked me.
>
> Maryam, 28 years old
>
> In Turkey I was treated very badly because of my veil... they don't like women wearing veils because they assume that we are from Saudi and they don't like Saudis.
>
> Sabah, 32 years old
>
> I've had the experience of living in Saudi Arabia and I can see the difference. I felt so much at peace there. I felt 'This is where I belong'. As soon as I'm here, it feels like we are at war, psychological war, a war of ideas, a war of culture, a war of our way of life. After living in England for eight years and then going to Saudi it was strange walking down the street and no one abusing me, nobody staring at me, nobody thinking I am the enemy. There we blend in so easily.
>
> Focus group participant

The notion of space highlights the relevance of obvious disadvantages to the process of victim selection. Indeed, space is one of the factors that make veiled Muslim women more or less vulnerable to Islamophobic victimisation. As Chakraborti and Garland (2012) observe in the context of hate crime, it is not someone's identity *per se* that renders them vulnerable but rather the way in which aspects of their identity intersect with other aspects of their self and with other situational factors and context including individuals' location. Green (2007) argues that the higher rates of victimisation amongst black and minority ethnic communities are relevant to the area they live in, in addition to victims' ethnicity or race. At the same time, potential targets of hate crime may be less likely to become a victim by virtue of living at a greater distance from prejudiced neighbours or in less overtly hostile environments (Walters and Hoyle, 2012). This discussion coincides with our earlier contention

DOI: 10.1057/9781137356154.0007

that the interplay of identities with one another and with other personal, social and situational characteristics renders veiled Muslim women a vulnerable target in the eyes of the perpetrator. We will return to this issue when we examine the impact of Islamophobic victimisation upon victims, particularly in terms of their sense of vulnerability according to their location.

Islamophobia as a form of racism

Having considered the different forms of Islamophobic victimisation, it is important to draw out the differences between the different groups of participants. In this respect, a more revealing picture emerges when the findings are considered in relation to participants' previous experiences of victimisation. Prior to 9/11 participants' status as visibly practising Muslims did not raise the risk of abuse or violence. However, all respondents (with the exception of white British converts to Islam) reported that they were victims of racist attacks – often described by perpetrators as 'Paki-bashing' – in the 1980s and victims of Islamophobia post-9/11. For these participants, Islamophobic victimisation was understood as a 'new' form of racism on the basis that there was a shift from race to religion. While the 'old' racism was based on an explicit belief on biological superiority, the 'new' racism is based on notions of religious and cultural superiority (Allen, 2010a).

> We had racial abuse in the early 80s when we first came to England. I had people shouting 'Paki' and 'Go back to your country' but now it's more 'You are a terrorist' so the abuse changed from race to religion.
>
> Alisha, 44 years old

> In the early 70s there was a time when skinheads were about and once they basically set alight a whole street, cars, bins everything. We were all scared to go out of the house. For a few days we couldn't get out. Even the police were too scared to intervene.
>
> Dahab, 52 years old

> It reminds me of my childhood in Yorkshire and the abuse I got because of the colour of my skin. When I was a teenager I wanted to have white skin. I wanted to be like everybody else. I felt I didn't fit in but now I wouldn't take my veil off.
>
> Zohra, 43 years old

DOI: 10.1057/9781137356154.0007

> We used to live in Brixton. We used to get chased a lot by skinheads. We couldn't even go to the park. It was that bad.
>
> Sahar, 47 years old

Lambert and Githens-Mazer (2011) point out that 'Paki-bashing' has been replaced by 'Muslim-bashing' as a new dangerous street phenomenon. Whereas ten years ago perpetrators might have focused on black and Asian people as potential targets, now increasingly their primary focus for attack are Muslims. In light of the serious racist attacks that some participants had suffered, experiences of Islamophobic victimisation felt like 'history repeating itself'. However, the white English converts who took part in the study had very different experiences to the black and Asian respondents who were born into Islam. Converts to Islam spoke of the sharp contrast in people's behaviour towards them after they wore the veil. On one level, when a veiled Muslim woman is targeted the offender will not be aware of the ethnic identity of the victim; however, being white indicates that this person is likely to be a convert. From this perspective, white veiled Muslim women are routinely perceived as British converts and thus they are targeted for their decision to convert to Islam. In the eyes of their abusers, converts have supposedly betrayed the British values and the British way of life, as the following comments indicate.

> I used to live in Croydon and there were some guys making comments like 'You're a traitor going against the values of our country'. I'm English so I get more abuse because they see me as a traitor.
>
> Zoe, 27 years old

> They know I'm English. They can see my eye colour, it's blue. They can see the colour of my skin, it's white. They can hear my English accent. They can see my daughter, she's English. People think I've moved over to the dark side. For them Islam is the enemy.
>
> Sarah, 31 years old

> I never had any abuse before. It's definitely because of the way I dress. When I didn't wear it, people were treating me like a normal human being and now they treat me like I am sub-human. Now they don't see me as a person, they look at my veil and they've got this image in their minds that we are all terrorists and our religion is evil. I know the mentality. I'm English. I know what they're like.
>
> Lina, 42 years old

DOI: 10.1057/9781137356154.0007

In conclusion, this chapter has examined the nature of Islamophobic victimisation and considered the different forms of abuse that veiled Muslim women experience in public. The chapter described both 'visible' and 'invisible' manifestations of Islamophobia such as verbal and physical attacks as well as persistent staring and a sense of being ignored. The preceding discussion has shown that experiences of Islamophobic victimisation can take a variety of different forms which may not be recognised or acknowledged as serious or even Islamophobic *per se* unless seen in context as part of the broader processes of targeted abuse and hostility that feature within veiled Muslim women's everyday lives. The next chapter considers the consequences of this victimisation for veiled Muslim women, their families and wider Muslim communities.

Notes

1 Additionally, a couple of participants reported that they had been verbally abused on social networking sites such as Facebook and Twitter as well as blogs and chat rooms.
2 Maryam felt that although she wore the veil, people could still see her smile through her eyes. Similarly, many participants said that when they smiled, their eyes 'smiled' too.

DOI: 10.1057/9781137356154.0007

5
Impact of Islamophobic Victimisation

Abstract: *The research findings discussed so far have focused predominantly upon the nature of Islamophobic victimisation. In this regard, understanding Islamophobic victimisation as an ongoing pattern of harassment, abuse and violence rather than as isolated, one-off incidents, highlights that veiled Muslim women are locked in a circle of repeat and multiple victimisation. From this perspective, there are unique emotional, psychological and behavioural consequences for actual and potential victims. Everyday experiences of both explicit and subtle manifestations of Islamophobia produce, inter alia, feelings of inferiority, loss of confidence and self-esteem, depression, flashbacks, guilt and self-blame. Within this paradigm, Islamophobia and its attendant forms of abuse, violence and harassment are often seen as 'normal' and 'natural' which highlights the 'ordinariness' of Islamophobic victimisation in terms of how embedded it is in the lived experiences of veiled Muslim women.*

Zempi, Irene and Neil Chakraborti. *Islamophobia, Victimisation and the Veil.* Basingstoke: Palgrave Macmillan, 2014. DOI: 10.1057/978113735614.0008.

Implications for victims

Being a victim of any kind of crime can have devastating and long term impacts upon individuals including emotional, psychological, behavioural, physical and financial effects. But as a form of hate crime, Islamophobic victimisation can be particularly distressing and frightening for victims, their families and wider Muslim communities. Empirical studies of targeted victimisation emphasise the more severe impact for victims of hate crime when compared to non-hate victims (see also Williams and Tregidga, 2013; Garland and Chakraborti, 2006; Hall, 2005; Herek, Cogan and Gillis, 2002; McDevitt, Balboni, Garcia and Gu, 2001).

In addition to potentially suffering physical injury, victims of Islamophobia can be seriously affected emotionally. In this regard, there are distinct emotional harms associated with this victimisation. Throughout interviews and focus group discussions participants highlighted that they had low confidence and low self-esteem because of experiencing Islamophobia in public. They also pointed out that they were made to feel 'worthless', 'unwanted' and that they 'didn't belong'. For converts in particular, experiences of Islamophobic victimisation often left them feeling confused and hurt, compounding their sense of isolation. Seen in this light, Islamophobic victimisation disrupts notions of belonging whilst maintaining the boundaries between 'us' and 'them'. This highlights the immediate effect of Islamophobic victimisation which is to undermine victims' sense of security and belonging whilst the longer-term or cumulative impact is to create fear about living in a particular locality and to inspire a wish to move away (Bowling, 2009). In this way geographical spaces are created in which 'others' are made to feel unwelcome and vulnerable to attack, and from which they may eventually be excluded (Bowling, 2009).

> Everyone thinks we are the enemy. I feel that I don't have the right to be here. It crushes my self-esteem.
>
> Parveen, 24 years old

> Recently someone said 'Why don't you go back home?' People think that because I'm covered up I'm not British. How should I dress to be British then? Would you say miniskirts are a British way of dressing? I'm the sort of person who wants to be accepted and it knocks my confidence when people say these things.
>
> Yasmine, 28 years old

DOI: 10.1057/9781137356154.0008

We've been made to feel that we are totally unwanted. It's like we are a virus to the community.

Focus group participant

Participants also described feelings of shame, self-doubt and guilt. They referred to incidents of Islamophobic victimisation as 'humiliating', 'embarrassing' and feeling powerless to do anything about it. The following comments help to convey the sense of humiliation and embarrassment that veiled Muslim women might feel when experiencing Islamophobic victimisation in public, often in view of people passing-by who do not intervene to help them.

I feel humiliated and I feel totally alone even though there are so many people around. If somebody would speak up and say 'Leave her alone, it's up to her how she dresses' but nobody has ever come to my defence.

Kalila, 29 years old

Last year I went to visit my parents in Malawi so at the airport I was in a wheelchair and they made me get up, they really thoroughly checked me and I thought 'Why are they doing that? I am not hiding a bomb in my wheelchair'. It was quite humiliating to be searched like that.

Rafia, 45 years old

It is awful because when they do it, they all do it publicly. There are witnesses all over the place. People are looking but nobody does anything. Nobody says 'It is wrong'.

Karima, 36 years old

Relatedly, the fact that no one would normally intervene to help them had culminated in 'blaming the victim'. In this sense, participants felt responsible and 'guilty' for being attacked on the basis that they were 'different' and therefore they 'deserved to be abused'. At the same time, it is likely that self-blaming was a way of making sense of their victimisation. The notion of self-blame is illustrated in the following comments:

When you have someone abusing you like that, you automatically feel it's my fault because I'm wearing this.

Huda, 27 years old

In our religion, it is compulsory not to travel without a man. This is for the safety of women, it is not oppressing women as most people think. If I was with my dad nobody would attack me. They wouldn't try it. So I kind of feel it's my fault if I go out alone and get attacked.

Salimah, 22 years old

DOI: 10.1057/9781137356154.0008

> We feel we are causing a crime and we are not. We are just covering ourselves; that is not criminal. Well now it is criminal in France but it's not in this country.
>
> Focus group participant

Furthermore, throughout interviews and focus group discussions participants argued that taking the veil off felt like a sexual attack and as such it had a similar impact upon them. In brief, it is important to recognise that victims who have been through this experience describe feeling frightened, guilty, ashamed and depressed.

> Taking the veil off is equal to rape really. I was walking down the street in the local area [Highfields, Leicester] and there were three white men in their early 20s. They took my niqab off from behind. I tried to conceal my face with my scarf and then when I tried to retrieve my niqab they wanted to take a look at me. They bent down to see what I looked like and then they chucked it on the floor. I was still covering my face with my scarf and I just tried to hurry away without running. When I went round the corner I put it on and started crying.
>
> Maha, 40 years old

> Although I don't have any bruises to show from the assault, I am damaged and harmed inside as if have been sexually assaulted.
>
> Iman, 37 years old

In light of the profound negative impact this victimisation can have upon victims, respondents relayed that the emotional scars can last for a long time, and that when another incident took place they relived previous incidents of Islamophobic victimisation. As a result some participants suffered from depression, eating disorders such as loss of appetite, bulimia and anorexia, sleep pattern disturbances including insomnia and nightmares, and flashbacks and memory lapses. In this regard, the continual threat of abuse can be emotionally draining for victims who not only relive past incidents but also feel the need to be constantly on the alert, even to the extent that they might become paranoid. This shows that Islamophobic victimisation can result in a cumulative experience of psychological trauma and emotional burnout over time.

> Every time somebody shouts, swears or laughs at me I will relive previous incidents that have happened again and again.
>
> Yasmine, 28 years old

DOI: 10.1057/9781137356154.0008

I suppose it can make me a little bit paranoid. I always keep my phone ready in case something happens.

Omera, 22 years old

Moreover, several participants felt angry, upset and frustrated on the basis that they were attacked because of their affiliation with Islam. Hate crime studies have established both specific and generalised frustration and anger on the part of victims – towards the perpetrator and towards a culture of bias and exclusion (see also Williams and Tregidga, 2013; Craig-Henderson, 2009; Herek et al., 2002; McDevitt et al., 2001). This coincides with our earlier contention that Islamophobia has become embedded in broader patterns of an ideological fear and hostility towards Islam whereby policies have tried to eradicate the visibility of Islam in the West, for example through veil bans in European countries such as France, Belgium and Italy.

I get upset when people say to me 'Go back to your country' because this is my home. I was born here. If you send me back to Pakistan I'd be lost, seriously.

Iffat, 25 years old

We are born and bred here. Where do they want us to go? Where is our future?

We don't belong anywhere. We have no place. It's like we are not wanted anywhere. Sadly to say in Switzerland we can't have minarets or a veil in France.

Focus group participants

However, a couple of participants pointed out that such experiences made their faith in Islam stronger. From this perspective, Islam became a more salient and important marker of identity in response to experiences of anti-Muslim hostility in public. It increased in-group solidarity and identification with their religious identity. It also made participants more determined to continue to wear the veil in public. Brown (2001) observes that as Muslim identities have been constructed as 'Other' to Western European identities, an attempt to distort Muslim identities, or to suppress the symbols of these identities, often has the opposite effect; it strengthens these identities. In this context, an attack which is perceived by the individual to be motivated by hatred towards Islam may lead to 'Islam' becoming a more predominant part of the person's self-identity. For Castells (2004), this illustrates the notion of 'resistance identity' with which to oppose attempts for social, religious, cultural oppression or assimilation.

DOI: 10.1057/9781137356154.0008

Interestingly, many participants reported that Islamophobic victimisation was part of the Muslim God's plan to 'test' their faith. In line with the belief that this victimisation was part of Allah's plan, participants felt confident that He would 'reward' them in the afterlife for not giving up their Muslim identity despite the abuse that they suffered in the present life. This contributes to the sense of resilience that some victims of Islamophobia feel in light of the 'rewards' that they will receive in paradise such as meeting the Creator.

> If I was to be stabbed or have stones thrown at me for the sake of my religion I would feel proud because Allah is testing me. This person is just the means.
>
> Faridah, 36 years old

> Everything that is going to happen to me is known to Allah. He's planned it for me so I trust Allah that everything is within His plan. Once there was a man on a bike, I was walking on the street [in Leicester] and he ran into me on purpose. He could have gone round me but he didn't. He ran into me and just shouted 'Look where you're going'. I was bruised for days. I think of this sort of thing as suffering for the sake of religion.
>
> Rahimah, 26 years old

> This is part and parcel of being a Muslim. The first thing I learned when I became a Muslim is that there are many hardships. This is a test. We believe that there is a better life afterwards.
>
> Zoe, 27 years old

> We know that any abuse we get, we get it just because we practise our religion properly. We believe in the afterlife, we know that there will be rewards for us in jannah [paradise]. This is a small sacrifice that we have to go through. It is a means for us to gain something better in the hereafter.
>
> Focus group participant

Vulnerability and fear

Experiences of Islamophobic victimisation increased feelings of insecurity, vulnerability and anxiety amongst participants, particularly for repeat victims. Bowling (2009) states that repeated or persistent victimisation can undermine the security of actual and potential victims, and induce fear and anxiety. The distressing nature of Islamophobic victimisation, coupled with the frequency with which these acts were committed, had created high levels of fear amongst participants, especially when in public space. In line with the apparent exclusionary intent and impact

DOI: 10.1057/9781137356154.0008

of this victimisation, participants felt extremely wary in public with a great sense of danger, which is illustrated in the following comments:

> Every day I step out of my house I fear that I might not return.
>
> Iman, 37 years old

> When people abuse me I feel intimidated because I don't know where to go and there's no one actually there to help me. It is so frightening because I'm on my own and there's a group of them.
>
> Aliyah, 18 years old

> I do feel fear depending on where I am. Here [in Leicester] I know who my enemies are, I know where they are, so it's easier. If I were to go somewhere else I'll have more fear because I don't know that area. For example, when I go up North I know there's a lot more racism.
>
> Rahimah, 44 years old

A couple of participants stated that they felt 'lucky' because, unlike other Muslim sisters who had suffered serious incidents of physical abuse, they had only experienced 'low-level' manifestations of Islamophobia such as verbal abuse in public. Nevertheless, they knew that they themselves were equally vulnerable to physical abuse and as a result they were fearful for their safety in public.

> Abdulilah I've been lucky because I haven't been physically attacked yet.
>
> Omera, 22 years old

> I've been very lucky in that my experiences have only been name-calling.
>
> Halimah, 19 years old

> My friend went out in her niqab [in Barcelona] and a man let his dogs off the lead and the dogs were running after her. She nearly got bitten. She said it was a very horrible experience. I'm really shocked and hurt a sister had to suffer like that. They treat us worse than animals. Being chased by dogs, you feel you are going to die. She was running for her life. I'm fortunately that I haven't had anything physical but I feel for her as I think I could be the next person.
>
> Talibah, 33 years old

The threat of abuse has long-lasting effects for victims including making them afraid to leave their homes and feeling like social outcasts. As a result a common sensation cited by participants was that of panic attacks, worry, extreme anxiety and depression, which was said to derive from the fear of having to endure future victimisation. Such feelings of fear and anxiety sometimes manifested in physical symptoms including

DOI: 10.1057/9781137356154.0008

headaches and migraines, back pain and fatigue. Participants also emphasised that they never felt safe and therefore they always had to keep their guard up and be vigilant.

> I'm always cautious of what is happening around to make sure that I'm safe.
>
> Nadia, 29 years old

> I always role play it in my head 'Right, if somebody comes up to me what am I going to do? I'll do this, do that' whereas I should not be thinking that way.
>
> Alisha, 44 years old

Clearly, participants feared for their safety; however, this sense of vulnerability depended upon particular spaces and places. For example, participants felt safer in areas where the Muslim public presence was well-established by virtue of 'safety in numbers'. By contrast, in areas where the Muslim population was rather small, the sense of vulnerability as well as the risk of attack was perceived to be significantly higher. Hindelang (2009) observes that the ability of individuals to isolate themselves from people with offender characteristics affects the probability of victimisation. Mythen et al. (2009) found that the fear of abuse restricted Muslims' freedom of movement in public, use of community facilities and visits to 'hostile' areas. Similarly, Tarlo (2007) highlights the reluctance of both hijab and niqab wearers to visit areas in London where they will be in a sartorial minority. Essentially, participants' fear increased when visiting 'hostile' or unknown areas, and decreased in more familiar or Muslim-friendly areas.

This discussion demonstrates how the enactment of physical boundaries impacts upon 'emotional geographies' in relation to the way in which participants perceived the spaces and places inside and outside their 'comfort zones' (Hopkins, 2007). Rather than risk the threat of being attacked many actual and potential victims choose to retreat to their 'own' communities and as a result become reclusive. Unarguably, this limits the behavioural options and life choices of individuals as it determines their area of residence, their vocational pursuits and leisure activities, their mode of transport, and even their access to educational opportunities.[1] Ultimately, this reality has resulted in segregation in housing, transportation, education, employment and leisure activities. However, as Perry and Alvi (2012) point out, this is not a voluntary choice; rather it is the 'safe' choice. They explain that the potential for future victimisation creates social and geographical yet 'invisible' boundaries, across which members of the Muslim community are not 'welcome' to step (Perry and

DOI: 10.1057/9781137356154.0008

Alvi, 2012). From this perspective, Islamophobic victimisation acts as a form of emotional terrorism on the basis that it segregates and isolates Muslims, particularly in terms of restricting their freedom of movement in the public sphere and changing their patterns of social interaction. Ultimately, the fear of attack reinforces these emotional and geographical boundaries whilst promoting patterns of segregation between 'us' and 'them'. Correspondingly, the 'us-versus-them' mentality is apparent in the following comments:

> From the point of our [Muslim] community, there is suspicion towards non-Muslims. There's no doubt about it.
>
> We don't feel safe enough to go out there and integrate. We feel that everyone is the enemy apart from the Muslims.
>
> Focus group participants

Participants were conscious of the fact that the threat of Islamophobic victimisation was always present, regardless of their geographical location. Indeed, even in areas with a high Muslim population such as the area of Highfields in Leicester, participants still experienced incidents of abuse, violence and intimidation and as a result their sense of vulnerability was still significant – though not as high as it would be in a non-Muslim area. As such, participants were often reluctant to leave the house even in their 'comfort zone' because of fear of being attacked particularly on the street, in parks, in shops and on public transport in the local community. Several participants reported feeling afraid of stepping out of their homes, certainly on foot. To avoid future attacks, they negotiated their safety in public through avoiding walking on the street and using public transport as little as possible.

> I used to take the bus to go to college but I felt everybody was staring at me so I decided not to use the bus for a while. I just walk to college.
>
> Halimah, 19 years old

> I can't drive so I have to take the bus. I don't normally travel on the bus upstairs, I always go downstairs so that I can get off at any time. I always travel on the lower deck of the bus but on one occasion I did have to go upstairs. There were about five young lads at the back of the bus and I was sitting on my own. One of them came and sat next to me thinking it was a laugh to sit next to me. They didn't do anything or say anything but just the close proximity was enough to make me feel under threat. I got off at the next stop even though it was four stops away from where I wanted to get off.
>
> Nimah, 28 years old

DOI: 10.1057/9781137356154.0008

Some participants revealed that they learnt to drive and bought a car or hired a taxi so that they did not have to walk on the street or take the bus. But there is no indication from the data that those who used a car and those who had made more restrictions on their lives were less likely to be victims of Islamophobia. For example, a key finding was that participants faced hostility and abuse when driving. Correspondingly, other drivers or people walking on the street had shouted:

How can you see with that thing on?

Rasheeda, 41 years old

Who gives you permission to drive?

Shafia, 31 years old

If you can't see why do you drive?

Nazia, 50 years old

In light of this, the majority of participants had altered their lifestyle with the aim of reducing the risk of future attacks. Some participants mentioned 'no-go areas' where they would face an increased risk of abuse whilst others restricted their public travel to a minimum. Participants who lived in Muslim-dominated areas in the UK revealed that they very rarely ventured outside of their local community and as such they (and occasionally their families) had imposed very strict curfews upon them. In this sense, they felt sheltered from hostility that they would experience had they left the local community and even the house. That stated, several participants revealed that they would not normally leave their house unless they had to do 'emergency' shopping or to collect their children from school. Those with young school children felt extremely unsafe taking them to and from school. This resulted in some participants choosing to home-school their children.

I home-school my kids so that I don't need to leave the house.

Rafia, 45 years old

I was in town [Leicester City Centre] and a white man came up to me and threatened me with a knife. After this incident I restricted myself from going out. I've become more reserved and tend to stay in the house more whereas before I would go out a lot.

Wadiah, 40 years old

The constant threat of Islamophobic victimisation had forced participants to adopt a siege mentality and keep a low profile when in public in order to reduce the potential for future attacks. Allen (2010a) observes that veiled Muslim women often try to become less 'visible' and therefore less vulnerable by taking the veil off. In this sense, experiences of previous victimisation can lead to numerous strategies of identity management, often geared toward the need to publicly validate the self as 'safe' (Mythen et al., 2009). Throughout interviews and focus group discussions, participants reported playing down their 'Muslimness' through reluctantly removing their veils, speaking in English (preferably with a British accent to demonstrate their 'Britishness') and reducing the use of Urdu in all or certain public places. In this context, veiled Muslim women appear to manage impressions of their Muslim identity in public mainly through concealment with the aim to reduce the risk of violence (Ghumman and Ryan, 2013).

> I try to speak loud enough so that people understand that there is an English speaking person behind the veil. As soon as they hear that I speak fluent English it usually changes people's perceptions. I find that they don't carry on being horrible because I've showed them that I'm a normal person. Maybe I dress differently but I am one of them.

> I keep my English name to avoid prejudice. Having a Muslim name does not say who you are. It's just a name at the end of the day.

> The purpose of the niqab for the woman is to protect her but if the woman feels the veil will harm her, she is allowed to take it off.

> Focus group participants

Interestingly, focus groups participants shared ideas on how to stay safe including wearing colourful jilbabs, hijabs and niqabs instead of black ones. Given that the veil can be worn in a variety of colours and styles, it is possible that certain combinations may be perceived as less 'extreme' forms of veiling.

> I try to dress myself differently. What I tend to do is if I am in an area which is predominantly Muslim, I'm comfortable wearing my black cloaks so everything is black but if I go to a non-Muslim area, I have a range of different colour cloaks and cloak sizes. I wear different colours and sizes to non-Muslim people so I don't seem very black in the face.

> I wrap it in a different way, for example, taking the scarf and wrapping it over my face or maybe showing my nose, something like that, you know, trying different ways of doing it. Sometimes I get a coloured niqab rather than a black one. Black is usually seen as more hostile whereas if it is a pink or a blue one it looks more friendly so people might not realise that I'm veiled.

> Focus group participants

DOI: 10.1057/9781137356154.0008

However, some participants took the extra step in veiling by covering their eyes and wearing gloves in order to hide their 'Britishness'. This was a particularly useful tool for white British converts who felt vulnerable on the basis of being seen as 'traitors', at least in the eyes of their abusers.

> I've recently started covering my eyes as well. Because I have blue eyes people know straight away that I'm a revert so they will treat me worse. They think that I betrayed them by becoming a Muslim. I feel more confident actually covering my eyes. I also wear gloves to avoid showing the colour of my skin.
>
> Aleena, 28 years old

Aleena's comment is an illustration of how experiences of Islamophobic victimisation impact upon the way in which women express their 'Muslimness' particularly in relation to their outward displays of faith, body presentation and dress (Mythen et al., 2009). Within the present study, defensive tactics included efforts to appear less desirable as a victim such as downplaying their Muslim identity. As such, a couple of participants concealed their adherence to Islam by discarding their veils and wearing Western clothes in some or all public places in order to blend in more easily.

> In Islam you have to look after yourself and if you are going to be in danger, you must take it off. I didn't want to take it off but I have to think of my children now.
>
> Tashia, 45 years old

Taking the veil off seemed to be a promising strategy for helping participants to erase the perceived source of their vulnerability and as a result reduce the risk of future attacks. At the same time though, there was a price to pay – the disapproval of other Muslims, in some cases friends and family, who criticised them for not being strong enough to keep the veil on. Participants themselves often felt that they had committed a sin by taking the veil off. Consequently, this increased participants' feelings of isolation, self-blame and guilt.

> Since I took it off, it feels like I've committed a really big sin. I was fighting with my own demons. I should have fought back. I shouldn't have removed it.
>
> Tashia, 45 years old

> There are many occasions I do take it off but I feel that the local community, because they know me for so many years with the veil, they think 'Oh, why is she not wearing it?' So for that reason, if I go somewhere where there are people from our [Muslim] community I will not take it off.
>
> Mahmooda, 27 years old

DOI: 10.1057/9781137356154.0008

> When I took it off, the ladies who wore niqabs were quite horrible to me. They judged me for taking it off. They said 'Oh, that's come off, so does that mean that everything else is coming off?' They said that in a very nasty way and I thought 'Is that what Islam teaches you?'
>
> Yara, 26 years old

Furthermore, defensive tactics included efforts to appear too formidable such as walking with a male companion. In this regard, acquiring strategies of resilience are presented as a means of preventing future victimisation. As we would expect from the earlier discussion of Islamophobia as a form of emotional terrorism – on the basis that it segregates and isolates 'visible' Muslims in certain or all public places – the fear of future attacks had restricted participants' freedom of movement, especially in the absence of other family members. As the comments below indicate, having a male companion was often reassuring as a form of protection against possible attacks. For some participants, even having their children with them made a difference. However, others felt confident enough to leave the house on their own.

> I know it sounds really sad but I don't want to go out alone. I prefer my husband to be with me or even my children.
>
> It depends on where I go because in familiar areas I can go on my own but if I go somewhere else I normally take my husband or my father.
>
> I don't always go out with someone else. I'm very brave. I can't keep waiting for everybody. I have things to do but I know sisters who wouldn't go out on their own.
>
> Focus group participants

At the same time though, not every participant had a male companion. For example, Haleemah felt extremely vulnerable as a single Muslim woman. She explained that wearing the veil seemed to be an obstacle for finding a (Muslim) husband as prospective partners told her that she would have to take her veil off if she wanted to get married. This infers that the wearing of the veil is often perceived as an 'extreme' form of practising Islam for 'moderate' Muslims.

> I'm more vulnerable because I don't have a male partner walking along with me. Single women like me, we don't have men accompanying us even to the local shops. Most of the time, there are women who are wearing veils but they have their husbands who are accompanying them so other people will not give them any abuse.
>
> Haleemah, 32 years old

DOI: 10.1057/9781137356154.0008

Furthermore, participants made reference to changing patterns of social interaction which often culminated in isolation and withdrawal. As Hindelang (2009) points out, for an experience of victimisation to occur, the prime actors – the offender and the victim – must have the occasion to intersect in time and space. By removing themselves from the public space or by reducing the time spent in public places, participants reduced the probability of Islamophobic victimisation. Accordingly, participants spoke of feeling safe by confining themselves to their home as much as possible, as this provided them with immutability from being attacked in public. Many participants explained that they would only go out if it was deemed absolutely necessary. In this case the home was understood as a retreat from the hostility of the outside world and a key source of personal sense of security (Magne, 2003).[2] From this perspective, the tangible fear of being assaulted limits pivotal aspects of identity building such as visiting friends, going to university and attending the mosque (Mythen et al., 2009). As such, the threat of violence deprived victims of freedom of movement and engagement (Perry, 2005).

In light of this, a couple of participants reported feeling like 'prisoners in their own home'. Although the experience and fear of victimisation had led those participants to withdraw from wider social participation, this was seen as the 'only way' to decrease their sense of vulnerability as they felt that there was nowhere else that they could be safe from the threat of abuse. Seen in this context, negotiations of personal safety can create a sense of imprisonment on the basis that they restrict veiled Muslim women's participation in society, despite decreasing exposure to Islamophobic victimisation in public. Although our understanding of Islamophobic victimisation concentrates on predominantly verbal and physical abuse of veiled Muslim women by strangers in public places, participants who were victims of domestic violence or had experienced Islamophobic victimisation in the home were likely to feel that nowhere was safe for them.

> It stops me from going out. I only go out when it is absolutely necessary, for example, to go to the shops or for medical treatment.
>
> Latifah, 46 years old

> It feels like we are under house arrest. People have locked us up without realising it.
>
> Duniya, 27 years old

I got chased by a couple of lads [in Yorkshire]. They were calling me names as I walked past them. I carried on walking, they started chasing me so I started running and they ran behind me. I went into a shop but luckily they didn't follow me into the shop. Now I have agoraphobia. I'm afraid to go out. I left my job. I'm stuck at home really.

Asima, 42 years old

People are being hypocritical in their argument that women in veil are oppressed because they oppress us. We are stuck at home all day.

Focus group participant

Implications for the family

Experiences of Islamophobic victimisation coupled with the potential for future attacks affected and sometimes seriously damaged the quality of life of participants and their families. On many occasions participants' children were affected by this victimisation, especially since they were witnesses of such incidents. For young children, witnessing their mother being abused was confusing and extremely upsetting. For Muslim girls in particular, such experiences discouraged them from deciding to wear the veil.

I was on my own with my five year old daughter in London, going to get the bus so I was crossing the road. A man in a big car, it was an English man in his 50s, pulled down his window and shouted swear words. Then my daughter started crying. She kept talking about it all day saying 'Why was that man so horrible mummy?'

Nadia, 29 years old

The incident at Sainsbury's [a white English man shouted 'Get the fuck out of my country'], my children witnessed it and my younger daughter was very upset because she couldn't understand why it happened. She was like 'Why is he saying that mummy? We are British, aren't we?'

Aisha, 34 years old

My daughters don't want to practise the veil. They are afraid because they see all the abuse I get when we are in town [Leicester City Centre].

Raniyah, 48 years old

In some instances the impact of Islamophobic victimisation was more profound for those participants concerned about the safety and wellbeing of their children. The process of victimisation experienced by participants often

DOI: 10.1057/9781137356154.0008

restricted their freedom in terms of their willingness to allow themselves and their families to visit certain parts of their local area or even to set foot outside their own house through fear of attack in public. In this regard, both the experience and threat of Islamophobic attack in public created a fear of leaving the house for both victims and their families. For many participants, the threat of ongoing or future attacks had resulted in them feeling compelled to make quite significant changes to their lifestyle patterns in order to protect themselves and their children; changes which almost inevitably compounded their sense of social isolation and withdrawal from their local community. At the same time, there were pressures upon participants from other family members to conform to and perform ascendant notions of 'safeness', including taking the veil off in specific or all public places and avoiding going out unless accompanied by a male relative.

> I had to go onto anti-depressants because I'm just so afraid to take my children anywhere. Why do I need my husband to take me to the park? I have to think of everything now like 'Is it safe to go out?' whereas before it wasn't like that. I feel like I'm stopping my children from doing stuff because I'm so afraid to go out.
>
> Yasmine, 28 years old

> When the last incident happened [a man ripped the veil off in Leicester City Centre] my dad said 'Don't you think you should remove it?' My husband is very supportive of my veil but my dad is very protective of me and he says that 'If you're going to put yourself into a situation where you're wearing the veil and it's going to make you vulnerable why are you doing it?'
>
> Iman, 37 years old

Participants emphasised the negative effects of this victimisation upon the male members of their family such as their father, brothers, husband and sons who felt inclined to protect them. Participants also discussed the risk of radicalisation particularly amongst young Muslim men who have grown up witnessing their mother, sisters or female relatives being attacked by virtue of being fully veiled in public.

> Muslim men feel that their women are under attack so they are going to feel very defensive. Women in Islam are held in high regard by the whole household and by the Muslim community.
>
> Nazia, 50 years old

> We are a close-knit community. Even if you're not married, you have a father, an uncle, a brother or a nephew who feels for you so it affects the male population too.
>
> Faridah, 36 years old

DOI: 10.1057/9781137356154.0008

My boys feel very angry. I think these things unfortunately drive young Muslim men to do things that they wouldn't normally do. When you're young, your emotions are all over the place and if somebody you respect and love is attacked, you would do things that you wouldn't normally do.

Lubna, 40 years old

Implications for wider communities

The emotional, psychological and behavioural impacts of Islamophobic victimisation are not restricted to victims and their families; rather, the harm extends to the wider Muslim community. This shows that Islamophobic victimisation affects not only the individual victim but also the collective victim. Correspondingly, the individual fear and vulnerability discussed above is accompanied by the collective fear and vulnerability of all Muslims, particularly those individuals who have a 'visible' Muslim identity.

Both Iganski (2001) and Perry (2001) point out that hate crimes are 'message crimes' whereby a message of hate, terror and vulnerability is communicated to the victim's broader community. Within this paradigm, incidents of Islamophobia send out a terroristic message to the wider Muslim community. In this sense, awareness of the potential for Islamophobic victimisation enhances the sense of fearfulness and insecurity of both actual and perceived Muslims. According to Perry's (2001) conceptualisation of hate crime as a mechanism for doing difference, the intent of hate crime offenders is to send a message to multiple audiences: the victim, who needs to be punished for his/her inappropriate performance of identity; the victim's community, who need to learn that they too are vulnerable to the same fate; and the broader community, who are reminded of the appropriate alignment of 'us' and 'them'. From this perspective, Islamophobic victimisation is directed toward the collective and not simply the individual victim. This emphasises the *in terrorem* effect of hate crime: intimidation of the group by the victimisation of one or a few members of that group (Weinstein, 1992).

Within the present study, several participants explicitly acknowledged the nature of their experiences of Islamophobic victimisation as 'message crimes'. As such, the 'message' was received loud and clear. Participants were conscious of the fact that they were liable to abuse, discrimination

DOI: 10.1057/9781137356154.0008

and harassment on account of their group identity as followers of Islam. Throughout interviews and focus group discussions the consensus view amongst participants was that the wider Muslim community is under attack by virtue of the fact that 'an attack on one Muslim is an attack on all'. For Muslims this is a crucial aspect of their faith; they are one body in Islam and 'when any part of the body suffers, the whole body feels the pain'. Respectively, Islamophobic victimisation is unique in the consciousness of the wider Muslim community through notions of a worldwide, transnational Muslim community, the ummah, which connects Muslims in the UK with other Muslims throughout the world. In light of the fear and hostility generated by 9/11 and 7/7, the consequential backlash against Muslims worldwide has strengthened this concept particularly amongst those Muslims living outside the Muslim world.

> You feel it as a whole. Whilst it is an attack on the individual, it's actually an attack on Islam as a whole. Therefore, it has an effect on everybody. We talk very much about the ummah, so any part of that which is attacked is felt across the whole community.
>
> Layla, 38 years old

> We feel we are all under attack. When it has happened to another sister or brother it does affect me. It affects all of us.

> In our religion, we believe we are all one body. If one person is hurt, it's like a part of our body is hurt so we all have to be concerned when women in niqabs are at risk.
>
> Focus group participants

In this sense Islamophobic victimisation is seen as an attack upon the fabric of the wider Muslim community. Moreover, Islamophobic victimisation also affects British society on the basis that it undermines the quintessential 'British' qualities of tolerance and multiculturalism that this country is proud of.

> We live in a democratic society and one of the beauties of British democracy is that people have the right to dress as they see best and this gives them a sense of pride. But when you have these incidents of violence it takes away that sense of tolerance that Britain prides itself on.
>
> Raniyah, 48 years old

DOI: 10.1057/9781137356154.0008

The normative aspect of Islamophobic victimisation

When considering the impact of Islamophobic victimisation upon victims, their families and wider communities, it is necessary to recognise that such incidents are far from being a single, homogenous entity. As our earlier discussion suggested, participants were multiple and repeat victims of both 'visible' and 'invisible' forms of Islamophobic victimisation. Rarely did participants describe Islamophobic victimisation as 'one-off' incidents; rather there was always the sense, the fear, the expectation for another attack. Crucially, recognising Islamophobic victimisation as a process signifies that it is 'part and parcel' of veiled Muslim women's everyday lives, and this reinforces the sense of constant risk for actual and potential victims. Within this paradigm, Islamophobia and its attendant forms of abuse, violence and harassment were seen by participants as 'normal' and 'natural'. This discussion highlights the 'ordinariness' of Islamophobic victimisation in terms of how embedded it is in the lived experiences of veiled Muslim women. Essentially, the fact that Islamophobic victimisation was understood as a normative part of the everyday lived experiences of veiled Muslim women also meant that some participants had become 'used to it' and therefore 'immune' to this victimisation. In light of the 'ordinariness' of Islamophobic victimisation, participants reported feeling weak, powerless and defenceless.

> If I have to go to town tomorrow I do expect people to give me dirty looks and make nasty comments. I expect it to happen. It really hurts me but what can I do? I've learned to live with it now. It's not affecting us anymore. We've got to that stage that it doesn't matter anymore.
>
> Huda, 27 years old

> It's part of life. I know I shouldn't be thinking this way but that is what's happening and there's nothing I could do about it.
>
> Samina, 35 years old

> It has become part of our lives and to some extent we have become immune to it. Nobody even talks about it because we're so used to it.

> I think when it happens, most of the time I expect it to happen. We face it so many times that we don't pay attention anymore. It doesn't really affect us because it is something we just learned to live with.
>
> Focus group participants

DOI: 10.1057/9781137356154.0008

As suggested in the comments above, Islamophobic victimisation was anticipated by participants to the extent that they had become 'immune' to it. This notion of immutability was coupled with a sense of helplessness on the part of participants. The majority felt that nothing could be done about it and therefore they would have to simply accept it and 'get on with things'. From this perspective, the inevitability of Islamophobic victimisation is tied with the passivity of victims; a notion of self-fulfilling prophesy. As such, there was a sense of fatalism in the general acceptance of the pervasiveness of targeted violence due to the visibility of their Muslim identity. This also infers a sense of resignation on the part of victims as it signifies the 'taken-for-grantedness' of everyday harassment and abuse (Perry and Alvi, 2012).

For the black and Asian women who took part in the study, this 'taken-for-granted' everyday harassment and abuse was relevant to past experiences of racist attacks. As mentioned in the previous chapter, some participants had experienced racism (prior to wearing the veil) within the context of similar incidents of verbal and physical abuse on the basis of their skin colour rather than their religion. These participants compared the impact of being physically abused or verbally abused as a 'Paki' or 'Black Paki' in the past with the impact of being physically attacked or verbally abused as a 'Muslim terrorist' in the present. For these participants, any one incident of Islamophobic victimisation added to the experiences of racism that their parents or they themselves had suffered whilst growing up in this country. Within this paradigm, the correspondence of the individual and the collective experience renders Islamophobic victimisation normative. It happened to their parents and now it happens to them, and therefore it is a 'normal' aspect of their lives (Perry and Alvi, 2012).

> My parents were very strong. They just got on with life as if it was just normal and we learned 'just deal with it'.
>
> I grew up in a white area in London knowing I'm different and compromising what I could and couldn't do. So when I put on the veil and people started making comments I knew how to cope with it. It makes no difference to me because I grew up looking behind my back. We are in England. We have to live with it.
>
> Focus group participants

This chapter offered insights into the lived experiences of veiled Muslim women as victims of Islamophobia in public places. It illustrated the

DOI: 10.1057/9781137356154.0008

seriousness of Islamophobic victimisation by outlining its nature and impact as experienced by veiled Muslim women themselves. The preceding discussion showed that the perpetrators reveal their motivation through the language that they use when verbally abusing their victims. In this regard, offenders commonly express their Islamophobic sentiments by way of an insult linking the victim to terrorism, although at times it is not clear whether the attacks are motivated by Islamophobia, sexism, racism, xenophobic sentiments or indeed a combination of these factors. However, according to participants' perceptions, the visibility of their veil is pivotal to these attacks, whilst perceived 'weaknesses' such as physical disabilities, language difficulties, ethnicity, age, physical shape and size increase the risk of being attacked. Having explored the ways and the frequency with which Islamophobia manifests itself in public, the chapter then outlined the consequences of this problem for victims, their families, and wider Muslim communities. Participants described the emotional, psychological and behavioural effects of this victimisation which in many cases had severe implications for their emotional and physical wellbeing.

Notes

1   For example, some participants were convinced that they would be discriminated against and this prevented them from pursuing a higher education degree.
2   However, some participants suffered from damage to their property such as windows smashing, persistent door-knocking, egg throwing and graffiti, and this had a cumulative effect upon themselves and their families. Attacks on property violate the security of the place where an individual is considered safest (Bowling, 2009). In this regard, the physical fabric of a house provides only an illusion of defence against attacks (Bowling, 2009).

DOI: 10.1057/9781137356154.0008

6
Conclusions and Reflections

Abstract: *In a post-9/11 climate, the visibility of the veil in the public sphere marks Muslim women as particularly vulnerable to Islamophobic victimisation. However, despite their vulnerability as actual and potential victims of Islamophobia, the lived experiences of veiled Muslim women remain 'silenced'. With this in mind, the aim of our work has been twofold: first, to examine the nature of Islamophobic victimisation directed towards veiled Muslim women in public places; and secondly, to explore the impact of this victimisation upon veiled Muslim women, their families and wider Muslim communities. This chapter takes stock of the key themes to have emerged from the research findings and offers a model of vulnerability of veiled Muslim women as potential victims of Islamophobia in public that recognises the interplay of different aspects of their 'visible' identities with other situational factors.*

Zempi, Irene, and Neil Chakraborti. *Islamophobia, Victimisation and the Veil.* Basingstoke: Palgrave Macmillan, 2014. DOI: 10.1057/978113735614.0009.

DOI: 10.1057/9781137356154.0009

Victimisation and the veil

Veiled Muslim women are routinely seen as oppressed, weak and powerless; such stereotypes marks them as 'easy' and 'soft' targets against whom to commit acts of Islamophobic hate and prejudice. As discussed in Chapter 1, popular perceptions of the veil as a symbol of gender inequality stem from colonial views of Middle Eastern women as exotic, subjugated 'other' women. Within the Orientalist framework, a sexual desire to see beneath the veil coupled with a colonial desire to 'modernise' veiled women paved the way for contemporary perceptions of the veil that portray veiled Muslim women as a homogenised group who are all forced to wear it. Seen in this light, veiled Muslim women form a collective group with a single identity. This notion of a collective identity ignores the meanings of the veil from the perspective of Muslim women themselves. For example, Muslim women choose to wear the veil as an expression of their devotion to Allah's commandments and for the benefits and advantages – perceived or experienced – which come from wearing it, namely, a sense of religious piety, public modesty and protection from the male gaze. However, both colonial and contemporary stereotypical understandings of the veil foster Islamophobia whereby Islam is depicted as a backward and misogynistic religion, Muslim women as oppressed and dangerous, and Muslim men as barbaric and violent. In this context, the veil emerges as a tool for identification upon which Islamophobia can be expressed.

In addition to gender oppression, the wearing of the veil is associated with self-segregation and the existence of parallel communities. In this regard, the veil hinders face-to-face communication and exacerbates the social isolation of veiled Muslim women because of the difficulty in communicating with a person whose face is covered. The wearing of the veil is also understood as a practice synonymous with religious fundamentalism and, as such, one which fosters political extremism. Seen in this context, the veil is linked to the 9/11 and 7/7 terrorist attacks and the global 'war on terror'. From this perspective, the covering of the face with the veil is seen as a 'threat' to public safety on the basis that the public have no idea who is behind the face covering – be it male or female. Taken together, these stereotypes provide the justification for Islamophobic attacks against veiled Muslim women as a means of responding to the multiple 'threats' of the veil as a symbol of gender inequality, self-segregation and Islamist terrorism.

DOI: 10.1057/9781137356154.0009

Chapter 2 illustrated that there are gendered dimensions to manifestations of Islamophobia in the public sphere. Within this framework, the gendered dimensions of Islamophobic victimisation are premised on five different, yet interrelated, arguments. First, stereotypes of veiled Muslim women as passive and subjugated render them 'easy' and 'soft' targets because of their perceived passivity and powerlessness. Secondly, the wearing of the veil provokes public manifestations of Islamophobia by virtue of its symbolism as a sign of self-segregation. Thirdly, the wearing of the veil represents the sexual non-availability of veiled Muslim women, and as a result their 'refusal' to conform to the expectation of being 'the object of the public gaze' challenges accepted gender norms. In this sense, veiled Muslim women may be attacked for failing to conform to Western expectations of how women should dress and behave in the public sphere. Fourthly, the image of the veiled Muslim woman represents 'Islam', the religion of the perpetrators of the terror attacks of 9/11 and 7/7. In light of this, veiled Muslim women are seen as 'responsible' for the actions of the terrorists. Therefore, attacks towards veiled Muslim women are justified because of the conflation of Islam with terrorism. Finally, veiled Muslim women may be targeted because they are seen as more visually 'threatening' than Muslim men on the basis that their Muslim identity cannot be mistaken, denied, or concealed. Collectively, the wearing of the veil marks Muslim women more readily visible as 'soft', 'easy', 'convenient' and 'appropriate' targets to attack when they are seen in public.

Using the city of Leicester as the research case-study area, the study employed a qualitative framework in order to examine the lived experiences of veiled Muslim women as victims of Islamophobia in public. As outlined in Chapter 3, the methodology included individual and focus group interviews with veiled Muslim women, individual interviews with local key stakeholders and policy-makers, and an ethnographic strand. A qualitative research framework was ideal for the purposes of researching the victimisation experiences of a 'hard-to-reach' group such as veiled Muslim women. Additionally, a qualitative analysis of the research findings facilitated the exploration of the themes which would have remained 'invisible' had the study relied on a quantitative approach. Such themes included the intersectionality of victims' multiple identities, previous experiences of racism and the significance of geographical location in terms of veiled Muslim women's vulnerability to Islamophobic attacks, to name but some. Chapter 3 also considered

DOI: 10.1057/9781137356154.0009

the role of the researcher as an 'insider' or 'outsider'. It was argued that being an outsider can benefit the research process (rather than obstructing it) by enabling the researcher to elicit detailed and in-depth responses, minimise participants' fear of being judged and maintain a critical distance from the interview data.

The analysis began in Chapter 4 with an examination of the nature of Islamophobic victimisation. The consensus view amongst participants was that the visibility of their Muslim identity made them a target. In this sense, the wearing of the veil made them identifiable as Muslims and as a result the abuse that they suffered in public was a direct implication of the visibility of their 'Muslimness'. When asked to describe the nature of victimisation experienced, participants suggested that the most common forms of Islamophobic victimisation were what are typically described as minor, 'low-level' types of harassment. This includes verbal abuse (such as name-calling, swearing and threats of physical violence), persistent staring, and a sense of being avoided by people. Moreover, participants stated they had experienced what would appear to be more serious forms of Islamophobic victimisation such as actual or attempted physical assaults. In terms of its frequency, experiences of Islamophobic victimisation were rarely 'one-off' incidents but instead part of a broader continuum of Islamophobia. Throughout interviews and focus group discussions, participants painted a picture of multiple and repeat victimisation over the course of their lives to the extent that it had become commonplace, normal and 'natural' for them. As a result, Islamophobic victimisation had come to be expected – and accepted – as an intrinsic part of their lives.

Experiences of Islamophobic victimisation had significant emotional, psychological and behavioural effects for veiled Muslim women, their families and wider Muslim communities. As discussed in Chapter 5, emotional and psychological impacts included feelings of depression, sadness, shame and guilt, as well as a reduction in confidence and self-esteem. Moreover, the risk of Islamophobic victimisation increased feelings of insecurity, vulnerability and fear amongst participants. Equally worryingly, participants described their sense of perpetual anxiety, which was found to derive from the fear of future victimisation as well as from the struggle to cope with the cycle of existing, everyday 'low-level' abuse in public. The threat of Islamophobic abuse had long-lasting effects for actual and potential victims including making them afraid to step out of their 'comfort zone'. Some participants reported feeling like 'prisoners in their own home' because they were afraid to step out of their house for fear of abuse.

DOI: 10.1057/9781137356154.0009

Along similar lines, the lived reality of Islamophobic victimisation seriously damaged the quality of life of veiled Muslim women's families, who often witnessed their mother, sister or wife getting physically or verbally abused in public by virtue of the visibility of her Muslim identity. The interview data also showed that manifestations of Islamophobia towards veiled Muslim women were perceived as an attack upon the fabric of the Muslim community itself. In this regard, Islamophobic victimisation was seen as a 'message crime' on the basis that 'an attack on one Muslim is an attack on all'. Essentially, Islamophobic victimisation is unique in the consciousness of the wider Muslim community through notions of a worldwide, transnational Muslim community, the ummah, which connects Muslims in the UK with other Muslims throughout the world. At the same time though, Islamophobic victimisation also affects the wider society because it undermines the fundamental values of liberal democratic states: the issues of choice, religious freedom and freedom of expression.

Understanding and responding to the vulnerability of veiled Muslim women

The research findings discussed so far illustrate that veiled Muslim women are likely to be verbally and physically attacked in public because of their affiliation with Islam, a religion and culture that is stereotypically associated with negative stereotypes, attitudes and perceptions. In addition to their Muslim identity, veiled Muslim women have many other 'visible' identities interwoven together including gender, ethnicity, age, socio-economic status (to name but some) which interact together. The interplay amongst these identities render veiled Muslim women even more susceptible to being perceived as a 'soft' target to attack. Indeed, the research findings revealed that veiled Muslim women are likely to be attacked because of the visibility of their Muslim identity, whilst signs of visible, perceived 'weaknesses' such as age, physical disabilities, mental health problems, language difficulties, and physical shape and size also increase their risk of victimisation in public.

Correspondingly, age was highlighted by the majority of participants as an intersectional factor that contributed negatively to how Islamophobic victimisation was experienced. For example, the veiled Muslim women who were very young or very old felt more vulnerable and as a

DOI: 10.1057/9781137356154.0009

result more fearful of being attacked in public. The findings from focus group discussions showed that those participants who were disabled felt more fearful of becoming victims of Islamophobia in comparison to the participants who were not disabled. In this case, they tried to conceal their disability where possible in order to minimise the risk of attacks. This is illustrated by Anisa, a participant who was partially sighted. Anisa decided to wear an eye veil (an extra layer of veil which covers the eyes) in order to conceal her disability despite the fact that this made it even more difficult for her to see in public. In addition, the research findings showed that there is significant intersectionality amongst race, ethnicity and Islamophobia. Accordingly, the black and Asian Muslim women who took part in this study revealed that they were sometimes subjected to verbal abuse which indicated both racist and Islamophobic hatred; for example, they were called names such as 'black suicide bomber'. The white British Muslim women who took part in the study were accused of being 'traitors' because they had converted to Islam.

Furthermore, the research findings showed that the vulnerability of veiled Muslim women as victims of Islamophobia can be influenced by local, national and global events. For example, participants who had worn the veil for many years stated that hostility towards them had increased significantly since the veil ban in France. Also, several participants felt that the risk of Islamophobic attacks increased whenever a high profile terrorist incident occurred in the UK or elsewhere in the world, and the media reporting identified the perpetrators as 'Muslim', 'Islamic' or 'Islamist' – a perception that offers support to the contention that terrorist attacks in the name of Islam bear influence on the frequency with which perceived or actual Muslims are victimised (Choudhury and Fenwick, 2011). There were also suggestions that the frequency of anti-Muslim hostility increased in instances when the EDL marches were in the media spotlight. Lambert and Githens-Mazer (2010) argue that post-9/11 certain sections of the media have promoted and encouraged Islamophobic sentiments whilst ignoring how readily Islamophobic comments can foster a climate in which violence against Muslims gains licence and tacit approval.

Equally importantly, the research findings demonstrated that location is another significant factor that makes veiled Muslim women more or less vulnerable to Islamophobic victimisation in public. In this regard, the veiled Muslim women who took part in this study felt that their sense of vulnerability was lower in areas with a large Muslim population whilst

DOI: 10.1057/9781137356154.0009

in areas with a small Muslim population there was a heightened sense of vulnerability to Islamophobic victimisation. Indeed, although Leicester is commonly perceived as a successful multicultural city, it is not immune to the problem of Islamophobia. Participants stated that the level of abuse that they suffered depended upon whether they were in their local community or whether they left their 'comfort zone', sometimes taking the bus to go to less familiar areas that did not accommodate 'difference' and Muslim 'otherness' in particular.

In hindsight, it is clear that there are certain spaces and places – even in a multicultural city such as Leicester – where veiled Muslim women might be at a heightened risk of attack and thus feeling more vulnerable. As Perry and Alvi (2012) note, the reality of Islamophobia creates social and geographical yet 'invisible' boundaries, across which members of the Muslim community are not 'welcome' to step. The enactment of physical, geographical boundaries impacts upon 'emotional geographies' in relation to the way in which Muslims perceive the spaces and places around and outside their communities of abode. Rather than risk the threat of being attacked, both verbally and physically, actual and potential victims opt to retreat to 'their own' communities. As a result, the majority of participants tried to avoid visiting areas where they would mix with non-Muslims. With these points in mind, Figure 1 shows that the vulnerability of veiled Muslim women to Islamophobic attacks in public places depends upon the visibility of their Muslim identity coupled with the visibility of 'other' aspects of their identity in parallel with other factors such as space as well as local, national and international events related to Islam, Muslims and the veil.

According to Figure 1, the likelihood that a veiled Muslim woman will suffer Islamophobic victimisation depends heavily upon on the intersections of religion, identity, 'difference', space and media reports of local, national or international events related to Islam, Muslims and the veil. Within this framework, for Islamophobic victimisation to occur several conditions must be met. First, the prime actors – the offender and the victim – must intersect in time and space. Secondly, the victim must be perceived by the offender as an 'easy' and 'soft' target to attack so that the perpetrator feels that he or she can 'get away with it'. Thirdly, the victim must be seen as 'deserving' the abuse so that the attack is justified, at least in the mind of the perpetrator.

Although it is important to recognise that the practice of veiling is *the* dominant motivating factor from a victim perspective, it is likely that the wearing of the veil in its own right does not necessarily make a

DOI: 10.1057/9781137356154.0009

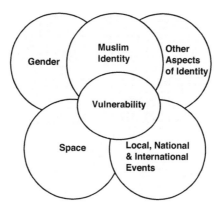

FIGURE 1   *A framework to explain the vulnerability of veiled Muslim women in public places*

Muslim woman vulnerable. Rather, it is how this identity intersects with other aspects of this woman's identity, such as being visibly disabled or elderly, and how this identity intersects with other situational factors, that makes her vulnerable in the eyes of the perpetrator. Acknowledging the interplay between these variables allows us to recognise that veiled Muslim women may be targeted not just for their group membership but because they are stereotypically perceived as 'soft', 'easy' or 'convenient' targets by virtue of the fact that they are visibly 'different' (through markers of dress, skin colour or language) and because they seem vulnerable (because of their gender, age,, disability or physical presence). At the same time, Islamophobic media reports of local, national or international events related to Islam, Muslims and the veil increase public hostility towards veiled Muslim women when they are seen in public, particularly in areas with a less established Muslim population. This intersection provides the perpetrator with the ability to attack veiled Muslim women in public.

This approach ties in with the suggestions of Chakraborti and Garland (2012) who argue that perceived vulnerability and 'difference', rather than identity and group membership alone can be targeted by perpetrators of hate crime. They propose that the intersections between a range of identity characteristics – including religion, race, ethnicity, disability, gender, age, mental health, bodily shape and appearance – are relevant factors in the commission of hate offences. This infers that the likelihood of being

DOI: 10.1057/9781137356154.0009

targeted is determined by the presence of factors that are distinct from an individual's 'main' identity characteristic. Within the context of this study participants were very aware that their experiences of victimisation were attributable certainly to their Muslim identity but also to their perceived vulnerabilities and 'difference', whilst location and media coverage also affected the likelihood of being subjected to Islamophobic victimisation. For us, therefore, the framework presented in Figure 1 has particular significance, both in drawing attention to the dynamics which contribute to the vulnerability of veiled Muslim women and the process of victim selection, and in painting a more complete picture of the lived realities of Islamophobic victimisation.

Correspondingly, this framework can be used by policy-makers and criminal justice practitioners seeking to understand and respond to the needs of veiled Muslim women as actual and potential victims of Islamophobia. The current 'one size fits all approach' is potentially flawed for veiled Muslim women as victims of Islamophobia on the basis that it does not take into consideration the intersectionality of victims' identities, nor the fact that veiled Muslim women may be more vulnerable in certain spaces and places, particularly in the aftermath of Islamophobic media reports of events related to Islam, Muslims and the veil. From this perspective, reforms must be made to provide 'at risk' victims with receiving support, tailored to the individual victim's needs. In this regard, religious and cultural sensitivity is crucial in offering high-quality support. Service providers need to be trained to deliver a service that is both faith and culturally sensitive. In addition, the significance of this model is that it is not only relevant to this particular study. Rather, we can apply these variables to other forms of hate crime victims. Indeed, this model can be used to explain the victimisation and vulnerability of other targets of hate. However, it is important to note that for the purposes of this particular study, the relevance of gender is implicit because it is only women who wear the veil. Ultimately, this analytic framework provides an important comment on how hate crime victimisation can be better understood as a consequence of this study. It is also important to provide adequate language services for recent immigrants who do not speak English because a language barrier can make the provision of services much more difficult. Existing physical disabilities and mental health problems should also be taken into account when offering support.

DOI: 10.1057/9781137356154.0009

Moreover, it is important that both policy-makers and criminal justice practitioners understand the diversity within the Muslim population which covers ethnicity, nationality and theology but most importantly, gender. Services need to be flexible to meet the needs of (un)veiled Muslim women and these differ considerably from those of Muslim men who have suffered Islamophobic victimisation. For example, access to female staff members is an important need for some Muslim women who will not otherwise access services. Similarly, the option of home visits by female police officers and support workers should be made available to veiled Muslim women who have been victims of Islamophobia. Additionally, while it is important that support service providers working with victims of Islamophobia recognise both the principles of the religion and the specific cultural backgrounds of those with whom they are working, it is also crucial that sensitivity does not stop there. Support service providers should develop the capacity and flexibility within their programmes to allow repeat victims to return to the organisation for additional and continued support. In cases where victims' needs are not fully recognised, a lack of appropriate support can add to the injury inflicted on the victim.

Ultimately, a lack of adequate support can be a source of distress, disappointment and frustration for those who experience it, as noted repeatedly by many of the women who took part in this study. It can make victims feel isolated, which can worsen the distress caused by the incident itself; it can result in victims electing to drop out of a case while it is being prosecuted; and it can impact upon the likelihood of crimes being reported in the future. At a point in time in which Islamophobic, anti-Muslim hostility is on the rise, providing effective support to veiled Muslim women as victims of Islamophobia seems more imperative than ever. Only by listening to their voices – and learning about their needs, their experiences and their expectations – can we begin to address both their vulnerabilities and their invisibility to the criminal justice system and society as a whole.

DOI: 10.1057/9781137356154.0009

References

Adler, P. A. and Adler, P. (2001) 'Reluctant Respondent' in J. F. Gubrium and J. A. Holstein (eds) *Handbook of Interview Research: Context and Method,* Thousand Oaks, CA: Sage.

Afshar, H., Aitken, R. and Franks, M. (2005) 'Feminisms, Islamophobia and Identities' *Political Studies* 53 (2): 262–283.

Ahmad, F. (2010) 'The London Bombings of 7/7 and Muslim Women in Britain – Media Representations, Mediated Realities' in F. Shirazi (ed.) *Images of Muslim Women in War and Crisis,* Austin, TX: University of Texas Press.

Ahmed, L. (1992) *Women and Gender in Islam,* London: Yale University.

Ahmed, N. M. (2012) *Race and Reform: Islam and Muslims in the British Media. A Submission to the Leveson Inquiry,* London: Unitas Communications.

Allen, C. (2010a) *Islamophobia,* Surrey: Ashgate.

Allen, C. (2010b) *An Overview of Key Islamophobia Research,* Birmingham: The National Association of Muslim Police.

Allen, C. and Nielsen, J. (2002) *Summary Report on Islamophobia in the EU after 11 September 2001,* Vienna: European Monitoring Centre on Racism and Xenophobia.

Allen, C., Isakjee, A. and Young, O. O. (2013) *Understanding the Impact of Anti-Muslim Hate on Muslim Women,* Birmingham: University of Birmingham.

Al-Saji, A. (2010) 'The Racialisation of Muslim Veils: A Philosophical Analysis' *Philosophy and Social Criticism* 36 (8): 875–902.

DOI: 10.1057/9781137356154.0010

BBC News (2005) *Hate Crimes Soar after Bombings*, http://news.bbc.
co.uk/1/hi/england/london/4740015.stm, (accessed 18 May 2011).

BBC News (2007) *Jury Sees 21 July 'Burka Escape'*, http://news.bbc.co.uk/1/
hi/6378863.stm, (accessed 16 November 2010).

BBC News (2010) *Damian Green Says Burka Ban Would Be 'Un-British'*,
http://www.bbc.co.uk/news/uk-10674973, (accessed 4 October 2010).

BBC News (2013) *Debate Needed on Veils in Some Public Places, Says
Minister*, http://www.bbc.co.uk/news/uk-politics-24104811, (accessed 20
November 2013).

Billaud, J. and Castro, J. (2013) ' Whores and Niqabees: The Sexual
Boundaries of French Nationalism Politics' *Culture & Society* 31 (2):
81–101.

Bowling, B. (1999) *Violent Racism: Victimisation, Policing and Social
Context*, Oxford: Oxford University Press.

Bowling, B. (2003) 'Racial Harassment and the Process of Victimisation:
Conceptual and Methodological Implications for the Local Crime
Survey' in B. Perry (ed.) *Hate and Bias Crime: A Reader*, London:
Routledge.

Bowling, B. (2009) 'Violent Racism: Victimisation, Policing and Social
Context' in B. Williams and H. Goodman-Chong (eds) *Victims and
Victimisation: A Reader*, Maidenhead: Open University Press.

Bowling, B. and Phillips, C. (2002) *Racism, Crime and Justice*, Harlow:
Longman.

Brown, M. D. (2001) 'Multiple Meanings of the Hijab in Contemporary
France' in W. J. F. Keenan (ed.) *Dressed to Impress: Looking the Part*,
Oxford: Berg.

Bryman, A. (2008) *Social Research Methods* (4th Edition), New York:
Oxford University Press.

Bullock, K. (2011) 'Hijab and Belonging: Canadian Muslim Women'
in T. Gabriel and R. Hannan (eds) *Islam and the Veil*, London:
Continuum.

Castells, M. (2004) *The Power of Identity* (2nd Edition), Oxford:
Blackwell.

Chakraborti, N. and Garland, J. (2012) 'Reconceptualising Hate Crime
Victimization through the Lens of Vulnerability and 'Difference'
Theoretical Criminology 16 (4): 499–514.

Chakraborti, N. and Zempi, I. (2012) 'The Veil under Attack: Gendered
Dimensions of Islamophobic Victimisation' *International Review of
Victimology* 18 (3): 269–284.

DOI: 10.1057/9781137356154.0010

Chakraborti, N. and Zempi, I. (2013) 'Criminalising Oppression or Reinforcing Oppression? The Implications of Veil Ban Laws for Muslim Women in the West' *Northern Ireland Legal Quarterly* 64 (1): 63–74.

Channel 4 News (2013) *More Than Half of Brits Want Full Face Veil Banned*, http://www.channel4.com/news/brits-back-ban-of-full-face-veil-niqab-poll-exclusive, (accessed 24 October 2013).

Choudhury, T. (2010) *Muslims in Europe: A Report on 11 EU Cities*, New York: Open Society Institute.

Choudhury, T. and Fenwick, H. (2011) *The Impact of Counter-Terrorism Measures on Muslim Communities*, Manchester: Equality and Human Rights Commission.

Commission on British Muslims and Islamophobia (2004) *Islamophobia: Issues, Challenges and Action*, Stoke on Trent: Trentham Books.

Council of Europe Parliamentary Assembly (2010) *Islam, Islamism and Islamophobia in Europe*, http://www.assembly.coe.int/ASP/XRef/X2H-DW-XSL.asp?fileid=17880&lang=EN, (accessed 22 January 2011).

Craig-Henderson, K. (2009) 'The psychological Harms of Hate: Implications and Interventions' in B. Perry and P. Iganski (eds) *Hate Crimes: The Consequences of Hate Crime*, Westport, CT: Praeger Publishers.

Craig-Henderson, K. and Sloan, L. R. (2003) 'After the Hate: Helping Psychologists Help Victims of Racist Hate Crime' *Clinical Psychology: Science and Practice* 10 (4): 481–490.

Dwyer, C. (1999) 'Veiled Meanings: Young British Muslim Women and the Negotiation of Difference' *Gender, Place and Culture* 6 (1): 5–26.

European Monitoring Centre on Racism and Xenophobia (EUMC) (2007) *Perceptions of Discrimination and Islamophobia: Voices from Members of Muslim Communities in the European Union*, Vienna: EUMC.

European Union Agency for Fundamental Rights (2009) *Data in Focus: Muslims Report*, Vienna: European Union Agency for Fundamental Rights.

Ferrari, A. (2013) 'A Besieged Right: Religious Freedom and the Italian War on the Burqa and the Niqab' in A. Ferrari and S. Pastorelli (eds) *The Burka Affair Across Europe*, Surrey: Ashgate.

Fernandez, S. (2009) 'The Crusade Over The Bodies of Women' *Patterns of Prejudice* 43 (3): 269–286.

Fielding, N. (2008) 'Ethnography' in N. Gilbert (ed.) *Researching Social Life* (3rd Edition), London: Sage.

DOI: 10.1057/9781137356154.0010

Keval, H. (2009) 'Negotiating Constructions of "Insider"/"Outsider" status and Exploring the Significance of Dis/Connections' *Enquire* 4: 51–72.

Khiabany, G. and Williamson, M. (2008) 'Veiled Bodies – Naked Racism: Culture, Politics and Race in the Sun' *Race and Class* 50 (1): 69–88.

Klaus, E. and Kassel, S. (2005) 'The Veil as a Means of Legitimisation: An Analysis of the Interconnectedness of Gender, Media and War' *Journalism* 6 (3): 335–355.

Lambert, B. and Githens-Mazer, J. (2011) *Islamophobia and Anti-Muslim Hate Crime: UK Case Studies 2010 – An Introduction to a Ten Year Europe-Wide Research Project*, London: European Muslim Research Centre.

Law, I. (2010) *Racism and Ethnicity: Global Debates, Dilemmas, Directions*, London: Pearson Education.

Leggatt, J., Dixon, C. and Milland, G. (2006) *The Veil is Banned in Hospitals, The Express,* http://www.express.co.uk/news/uk/1345/The-veil-is-banned-in-hospitals, (accessed 16 November 2010).

Liamputtong, P. (2009) *Qualitative Research Methods*, Melbourne: Oxford University Press.

Lutz, H, Phoenix, A. and Yuval-Davis, N. (1995) 'Nationalism, Racism and Gender – European Crossfires' in H. Lutz, A. Phoenix and N. Yuval-Davis (eds) *Crossfires: Nationalism, Racism and Gender in Europe*, London: Pluto Press.

Lyon, D. and Spini, D. (2004) 'Unveiling the Headscarf Debate' *Feminist Legal Studies* 12 (3): 333–345.

Mabro, J. (1991) *Veiled Half-Truths: Western Travellers Perceptions of Middle Eastern Women*, London: I. B. Tauris.

Macdonald, M. (2006) 'Muslim Women and the Veil: Problems of Image and Voice in Media Representations' *Feminist Media Studies* 6 (1): 7–23.

Magne, S. (2003) *Multi-Ethnic Devon: A Rural Handbook – The Report of the Devon and Exeter Racial Equality Council's Rural Outreach Project*, Devon: Devon and Exeter Racial Equality Council.

Malik, M. (2008) 'Complex Equality: Muslim Women and the "Headscarf"' *Droit et Société* 68 (1): 127–152.

MAMA (2013) *Making Your Voice Heard*, http://tellmamauk.org/main, (accessed 8 November 2013).

Mancini, L. (2013) 'Burka, Niqab and Women's Rights' in A. Ferrari and S. Pastorelli (eds) *The Burka Affair Across Europe*, Surrey: Ashgate.

DOI: 10.1057/9781137356154.0010

Maxfield, M. G., and Babbie, E. R. (2009) *Basics of Research Methods for Criminal Justice and Criminology* (2nd Edition), Belmont: Thompson.

McDevitt, J., Balboni, J., Garcia, L. and Gu, J. (2001) 'Consequences for Victims: A Comparison of Bias-and Non-Bias-Motivated Assaults' in P. Gerstenfeld and D. R. Grant (eds) *Crimes of Hate: Selected Readings*, London: Sage.

McGhee, D. (2005) *Intolerant Britain?: Hate, Citizenship and Difference*, Maidenhead: Open University Press.

Meer, N., Dwyer, C. and Modood, T. (2010) 'Embodying Nationhood? Conceptions of British National Identity, Citizenship and Gender in the "Veil Affair"' *The Sociological Review* 58 (1): 84–111.

Modood, T. (1997) ' "Difference", Cultural Racism and Anti-Racism' in T. Modood and P. Werbner (eds) *Debating Cultural Hybridity: Identities and the Politics of Anti-Racism*, London: Zed Books.

Mondal, A. A. (2008) *Young British Muslim Voices*, Oxford: Greenwood World.

Moran, L. and Sharpe, A. (2004) Violence, Identity and Policing: The Case of Violence against Transgender People *Criminal Justice* 4 (4): 395–417.

Mythen, G. (2007) 'Cultural Victimology: Are We All Victims Now?' in S. Walklate (ed.) *Handbook of Victims and Victimology*, Cullompton: Willan.

Mythen, G., Walklate, S. and Khan, F. (2009) ' "I'm a Muslim, but I'm not a Terrorist": Victimisation, Risky Identities and the Performance of Safety', *British Journal of Criminology* 49 (6): 736–754.

Open Society Foundations (2011) *Unveiling the Truth: Why 32 Muslim Women Wear the Full-face Veil in France*, London: Open Society Foundations.

Open Society Institute (2005) *Muslims in the UK: Policies for Engaged Citizens*, London: Open Society Institute.

Parekh, B. (2000) *The Future of Multi-Ethnic Britain*, London: Profile Books.

Perry, B. (2001) *In the Name of Hate: Understanding Hate Crimes*, London: Routledge.

Perry, B. (2005) 'A Crime By Any Other Name: The Semantics of Hate' *Journal of Hate Studies* 4 (1): 121–137.

Perry, B. and Alvi, S. (2012) ' "We Are All Vulnerable": The *in Terrorem* Effects of Hate Crimes' *International Review of Victimology* 18 (1): 57–71.

DOI: 10.1057/9781137356154.0010

Phillips, C. and Bowling, B. (2003) 'Racism, Race and Ethnicity: Developing Minority Perspectives in Criminology' *British Journal of Criminology* 43 (2): 269–290.

Raju, S. (2002) 'We Are Different, But Can We Talk?' *Gender, Place and Culture* 9 (2): 173–177.

Robert, N. (2005) *My Sisters' Lips: A Unique Celebration of Muslim Womanhood*, London: Bantam Press.

Runnymede Trust (1997) *Islamophobia: A Challenge for us All*, London: Author.

Said, E. (1981) *Covering Islam: How the Media and Experts Determine How We See the Rest of the World*, London: Routledge.

Sallah, M. (2010) *The Ummah and Ethnicity: Listening to the Voices of African Heritage Muslims in Leicester*, Leicester: Leicester City Council.

Scott-Baumann, A. (2011) 'Unveiling Orientalism in Reverse' in T. Gabriel and R. Hannan (eds) *Islam and the Veil*, London: Continuum.

Shackle, S. (2013) *Why Would Anyone Believe in the 'Islamophobia Industry'? The NewStatesman,* http://www.newstatesman.com/uk-politics/2013/10/why-would-anyone-believe-islamophobia-industry, (accessed 3 October 2013).

Shah, S. (2004) 'The Researcher/Interviewer in Intercultural Context: A Social Intruder!' *British Educational Research Journal* 30 (4): 549–575.

Spalek, B. (2002) *Islam, Crime and Criminal Justice,* Cullompton: Willan.

Spalek, B. (2005) 'A Critical Reflection on Researching Black Muslim Women's Lives Post-September 11th' *International Journal of Social Research Methodology* 8 (5): 405–418.

Stokes, P. (2006) *Murder Suspect Fled Under Muslim Veil, The Telegraph,* http://www.telegraph.co.uk/news/uknews/1537414/Murder-suspect-fled-under-Muslim-veil.html, (accessed 12 November 2010).

Tarlo, E. (2007) 'Hijab in London: Metamorphosis, Resonance and Effects' *Journal of Material Culture* 12 (2): 131–156.

The Independent (2013) *EDL Marches on Newcastle as Attacks on Muslims Increase Tenfold in the Wake of Woolwich Machete Attack Which Killed Drummer Lee Rigby,* http://www.independent.co.uk/news/uk/crime/edl-marches-on-newcastle-as-attacks-on-muslims-increase-tenfold-in-the-wake-of-woolwich-machete-attack-which-killed-drummer-lee-rigby-8631612.html, (accessed 25 May 2013).

Tinker, C. and Armstrong, N. (2008) 'From the Outside Looking in: How an Awareness of Difference Can Benefit the Qualitative Research Process' *The Qualitative Report* 13 (1): 53–60.

DOI: 10.1057/9781137356154.0010

Tissot, S. (2011) 'Excluding Muslim Women: From Hijab to Niqab, from School to Public Space' *Public Culture* 23 (1): 39–46.

Tourkochoriti, I. (2012) 'The Burka Ban: Divergent Approaches to Freedom of Religion in France and in the U.S.A.' *William and Mary Bill of Rights Journal* 20: 791–852.

Tyrer, D. and Ahmad, F. (2006) *Muslim Women and Higher Education: Identities, Experiences and Prospects*, Oxford: Oxuniprint.

Vakulenko, A. (2007) 'Islamic Headscarves and the European Convention On Human Rights: an Intersectional Perspective' *Social and Legal Studies* 16 (2): 183–199.

Walters, M. A. and Hoyle, C. (2012) 'Exploring the Everyday World of Hate Victimisation through Community Mediation' *International Review of Victimology* 18 (1): 7–24.

Weller, P. (2011) *Religious Discrimination in Britain: A Review of Research Evidence, 2000-10*, London: Equality and Human Rights Commission.

Weinstein, J. (1992) 'First Amendment Challenges to Hate Crime Legislation: Where's the Speech?' *Criminal Justice Ethics* 11 (2): 6–20.

Williams, M. and Tregidga, J. (2013) *Time for Justice: All Wales Hate Crime Research Project*, Cardiff: Race Equality First.

Yegenoglu, M. (1998) *Colonial Fantasies: Towards a Feminist Reading of Orientalism*, Cambridge: Cambridge University Press.

Young, A. (2004) 'Experiences in Ethnographic Interviewing about Race: The Inside and Outside of it' in M. Bulmer and J. Solomos (eds) *Researching Race and Racism,* London: Routledge.

YouGov (2013) *Most Still Want To Ban The Burka in Britain*, http://yougov.co.uk/news/2013/09/18/most-still-want-ban-burka-britain/, (accessed 18 September 2013).

Zebiri, K. (2008) 'The Redeployment of Orientalist Themes in Contemporary Islamophobia' *Studies in Contemporary Islam* 10: 4–44.

DOI: 10.1057/9781137356154.0010

Index

DOI: 10.1057/9781137356154.0011

DOI: 10.1057/9781137356154.0011

DOI: 10.1057/9781137356154.0011